MIDDLE EAST RULES OF THUMB

MIDDLE EAST RULES OF THUMB

Understanding the complexities of the Middle East

A handbook
Second Edition

Steven Carol
Author of
Encyclopedia of Days:
Start the Day with History

iUniverse, Inc.
New York   Bloomington

MIDDLE EAST RULES OF THUMB
Understanding the Complexities of the Middle East
Second Edition

Copyright © 2008-2009 by Steven Carol

All rights reserved. No part of this book may be used or reproduced by any means, graphic, electronic, or mechanical, including photocopying, recording, taping or by any information storage retrieval system without the written permission of the publisher except in the case of brief quotations embodied in critical articles and reviews.

iUniverse books may be ordered through booksellers or by contacting:

iUniverse
1663 Liberty Drive
Bloomington, IN 47403
www.iuniverse.com
1-800-Authors (1-800-288-4677)

Because of the dynamic nature of the Internet, any Web addresses or links contained in this book may have changed since publication and may no longer be valid.

The views expressed in this work are solely those of the author and do not necessarily reflect the views of the publisher, and the publisher hereby disclaims any responsibility for them.

This book's relevance to the current Middle-East crisis is based on hard, carefully researched, facts. Although the region faces constant uncertainty, the principles outlined in this book are valid and timeless. This book should accompany any examination of information appearing in the media. News, editorials, and popular literature on this highly-controversial subject are often plagued by inaccurate information, or even disinformation. Anyone who wishes to understand the complex problems at hand, and especially those who wish to comment or write about them, will greatly benefit from this book. It will prevent them from making common and not so common mistakes for lack of adequate knowledge.

ISBN: 978-0-595-48235-1 (pbk)
ISBN: 978-0-595-48758-5 (cloth)
ISBN: 978-0-595-60327-5 (ebk)

iUniverse Rev Date 11/14/2008

Printed in the United States of America

To Hadara for her encouragement, support and love.
To Shelli and David, with love for them and their posterity.

I wish to thank Eddie and Joan for their generous assistance in helping make this work possible and to Michael, Kobe, and Bill for their editorial and technical assistance in preparation of this work.

Table of Contents

Tables X
Geography 1
Demography 5
Tradition/History 9
Islam 19
Politics 27
Alliances 36
War 38
Negotiations 60
Security 73
Media 78
Conclusion 85
Appendix 1—Vital waterways 87
Appendix 2—Etymological history of the terms "Near East" and "Middle East" 93
Appendix 3—The Eisenhower Doctrine (annotated) 99
Appendix 4—A short history of Israel 101
Appendix 5—Population exchanges and transfers 107
Appendix 6—Mandatory Palestine land facts 111
Appendix 7—The Balfour Declaration (annotated) 115
Appendix 8—A second Palestinian state? 117
Appendix 9—A territorial comparison 119
Appendix 10—The Palestinian National Covenant (annotated), the Islamic Resistance Movement-the Hamas Covenant, and Fatah Constitution 121

Appendix 11—The spread of Islam 135

Appendix 12—Time line of Islam, Muslim conquests and
setbacks 137

Appendix 13—The Arab (Jordanian) occupation of Jerusalem
1948-1967 151

Appendix 14—Some historic occupations 155

Appendix 15—*Dhimmi* status 159

Appendix 16—Famous Kings, Queens and Pharaohs of Egypt.... 163

Appendix 17—The League of Arab States 167

Appendix 18—Judea and Samaria 169

Appendix 19—Israel's insecure borders, 1949-1967,
and soon again? 173

Appendix 20—The Jewish connection to Jerusalem 175

Appendix 21—The Constantinople Convention on Free Navigation
of the Suez Canal 181

Appendix 22—Egyptian President Gamal Abdel Nasser
nationalizes the Suez Canal, July 26, 1956 (annotated) 183

Appendix 23—UN "Zionism is Racism" resolution
and its repeal 189

Appendix 24—UN General Assembly Resolution 181–Palestine
partition plan of 1947 (annotated) 195

Appendix 25—United Nations Security Council Resolutions 242
(1967) and 338 (1973) 201

Appendix 26—Jewish population in Arab countries 205

Suggested Reading 206

Internet Resources 246

About the Author 253

Index 257

TABLES

Annual contributions to UNRWA (2000) 7
Status of women under *sharia* (Islamic law) 23
Nile River vs. Tigris-Euphrates Rivers rivalry 30
Attempts at Pan-Arab unity 31
Modern conflict in the Middle East (excluding the Arab-Israel conflict) 40
The war of words 82
Suez Canal historic time-line 88
Sailing distances with and without use of the Suez Canal 89
A short history of Israel 101
Time-line of Islam, Muslim conquests and setbacks 137
Recent examples of continued Muslim expansion 147
Some historic occupations 155
Famous kings, queens, and pharaohs of Egypt 163
Members of the Arab League 167
UN partition of Palestine 1947–land and people 195

FOREWORD

It is my pleasure to recommend to you Professor Carol's new book. These are not "rules of thumb" to remember, as no one has such a good memory. This book is actually a compilation of hard, extremely carefully researched, facts relevant to the current Middle-East crisis. One must, therefore, not forget to use this book when examining information that appears in the media or in other books on the subject. Readers will be surprised at the amount of inaccurate information, or even disinformation, one encounters in the news, editorials or popular literature about this highly controversial field.

The facts presented by Professor Steven Carol in a well organized fashion, were researched and rechecked by Professor Carol, a well recognized expert on modern Middle Eastern and African history.

The author's original intent might have been to give a reader of current events on Israel and its neighborhood a set of hard facts to help avoiding the traps of Arab propaganda and anti-American and anti-Israeli media bias. However, what has resulted is a hefty volume of information hardly available elsewhere without many hours of tedious academic research.

Unlike other authors on the subject, which has become highly popular lately, Professor Carol is a perfectionist who makes sure that the information he provides is accurate, and therefore reliable. Anyone who wishes to understand the complex problems at hand,

and especially those who wish to comment or write about them, will greatly benefit from this book. It will prevent them from making common, and not so common, mistakes for lack of adequate knowledge.

The author's strong opinions are backed by the facts, which by themselves, constitute highly reliable information. Therefore, this book is very likely to become the gold standard on the subject. Moreover, it will not be readily dated, like many other books in the field, because the facts compiled here will remain valid and immutable.

In brief, anyone sincerely interested in this subject will find in this volume highly useful information and material for thought.

Prof. Michael Anbar Ph.D.
Professor Emeritus,
University at Buffalo
Author of Israel and its Future

PREFACE

During the course of a teaching career of nearly four decades, having written numerous articles about the subject, being a consultant about the Middle East, and now being involved with a radio show dealing with the Middle East, it has become obvious to me, as it has to others, that understanding the complexities of Middle East history, politics, diplomacy and culture can be confusing. This is due in large part to the mainstream media's policy of printing propaganda as "news," and continually committing the sin of "omission"–leaving out important information that can help a reader/listener comprehend the entire picture.

In an effort to provide clarity, I have put together a series of what I term "Rules of Thumb" about relevant topics. It is my hope that the reader will gain insight by applying these when hearing or reading news or commentaries on these subjects.

For most effective use of this work, each "rule" has examples. Additionally there are appendices that provide more comprehensive material. The "rule" and appendix, where mentioned, are designed to be utilized in tandem and concurrently.

An alternative, effective way to use this book is to start with the index, look up the name or term of interest, and then consult the text for detailed information.

Dr. Steven Carol
December 2008

NOTE ON CALENDARS

All dates in the chronologies and the body of the book are given in the calendar traditionally referring to events before the birth of Jesus (BC) and continuing after his birth (AD), and now universally adopted and known to scholars as Before the Common Era (BCE) and the Common Era (CE).

MIDDLE EAST RULES OF THUMB

GEOGRAPHY

1. No other region of the world has such importance throughout history to the present day.

The Middle East is the cradle of civilization. Some of the earliest recorded societies grew in the Nile River Valley and in the Tigris-Euphrates Valley. Ancient civilizations, including the Akkadians, Sumerians, Phoenicians, Hebrews, Babylonians, and Egyptians had their origins there. The region is the birthplace of the three monotheistic faiths: Judaism, Christianity and Islam.

The Middle East has immense geographic importance being the land bridge to three continents–Europe, Asia and Africa. Throughout history invasion routes have passed through the region. It contains water routes of immense importance, geographically, economically, historically, and politically–the Nile, Tigris, and Euphrates, as well as the Shatt al-Arab, the 125-mile confluence of the Tigris and Euphrates that flows into the Persian Gulf. Five of the most important straits in the world are located in the region: The Dardanelles, the Bosporus, Tiran, Bab el-Mandeb and Hormuz. In addition one of the great maritime highways, the Suez Canal, is situated in the area (See Appendix 1–Vital Waterways). Not to be overlooked are the vast reserves of petroleum located in the region.

2. The terms "Middle East" and "Near East" continue to be used interchangeably.

Prior to 1954, the term "Near East" was used extensively, and generally referred to an area bounded by Egypt in the west, Iraq on the east, Turkey to the north, and extended to the southern tip of the Arabian Peninsula. From 1954 on, "Middle East" became the prevalent description, though it has not been exclusive.

The geographic parameters of the region have also broadened, frequently including the area from Libya on the west to Iran on the east, from Turkey in the north to the southern tip of the Arabian Peninsula, including Sudan on northeastern Africa. The broadest description incorporates Mauritania and Morocco in the west to Iran in the east, and Turkey in the north down to the Horn of Africa in the south. (For more details, see Appendix 2–Etymological history of the terms "Near East" and "Middle East.")

Currently the State Department has a Bureau of Near East Affairs dealing with Algeria, Bahrain, Egypt, Iran, Iraq, Israel, Jordan, Kuwait, Lebanon, Libya, Morocco, Oman, Qatar, Saudi Arabia, Syria, Tunisia, United Arab Emirates, and Yemen. Similarly, the American Israel Public Affairs Committee for over half a century has published a bi-weekly newsletter called the "Near East Report."

However, the Middle East Institute in Washington, D.C. defines the Middle East as southwestern Asia and northeastern Africa, from Mauritania and Morocco to Pakistan, including the Caucasus and Central Asian republics of Kazakhstan, Kyrgyzstan, Uzbekistan, Turkmenistan, and Tajikistan.

3. Middle East countries have been "created" but Israel isn't one of them.

Libya, Sudan, Jordan, Syria, Lebanon, and Iraq all were "created" by Great Britain, France, and Italy. Saudi Arabia was "created" by force by one man, King Abd al-`Azīz ibn Abdur Rahman Al-Feisal Āl Sa`ūd (commonly known as ibn Saud) in 1932. Israel, in contrast, was re-established as a sovereign nation in the very land where two previous Jewish sovereign polities had existed before they were conquered by outside aggressors (See Appendix 4–A Short History of Israel).

4. Distance in the Middle East IS of importance.

For example the Old City of Jerusalem is less than a kilometer across. For tiny countries such as Bahrain, Qatar, Kuwait, Cyprus, Lebanon, and Israel distance is existentially critical. Every kilometer can be argued over–and in many cases fought over. As recent history has shown, a tiny country can be invaded and occupied quickly. When larger countries claim, in a cavalier-like fashion, that "another kilometer here or there does not count, in this age of missile technology," they are being less than honest with someone else's territory. Such cessions of kilometers may prove fatal for a small country.

5. Geographic denial, omissions and substitutions are prevalent on Arab/Muslim maps of the region.

One will not find "Israel" indicated on maps in the Arab/Muslim world. What will be found where Israel has been located for sixty years, is a non-existent country called "Palestine" or the entire area, from the Mediterranean Sea to the Jordan River, labeled "Occupied Territory of Palestine." In a similar vein Syrian maps do not show a separate independent nation of Lebanon, nor Iskenderun, (formerly known as Alexandretta) as part of Turkey–but rather Syrian. The Iranian province of Khuzistan does not exist, only Arabistan is inscribed on Arab maps, and the Persian Gulf is not found, but it is named the "Arabian Gulf."

DEMOGRAPHY

6. Contrary to the claim that the Middle East is exclusively Arab, the region has been, and continues to be, inhabited by other peoples, most of whom pre-date the Arabs, who emerged from the Arabian Peninsula in the 7th century.

These peoples include the Berbers, Turks, Kurds, Jews, Persians, Armenians, Azeris, Turkomans, Baluchis, and Circassians.

7. Another claim made is that the so-called "Arab Middle East" is exclusively Muslim. This too is a falsehood. Other faiths have existed in the region, most of them pre-dating the advent of Islam.

These include: Greek Orthodox, Nestorians (Assyrians), Coptic Orthodox, Jacobite (Syrian) Orthodox, Armenian Orthodox, Roman Catholics, Armenian Catholics, Greek Catholics, Syrian Catholics, Chaldean Catholics, Coptic Catholics, Maronites, numerous Protestant denominations, Druze, Rabbinical Jews and members of other Jewish sects, Karaites, Samaritans, Yezids, Mandaneans, Shabaka, Bahais, Zoroastrians, and Animists.

8. The "refugee problem" connected with the Arab-Israeli conflict, is not one of "Palestinian Arab" refugees alone. It is a twin refugee problem, which needs to be addressed and solved by both parties to the conflict.

As a result of the 1948-1949 Arab invasion of Israel, 650,000 Arabs (UN statistics) fled Israel, while 160,000 remained in the Jewish state. At the same time Jews living in Arab countries were attacked and expelled. Between 1948 and 1976 over 880,000 Jews had been driven out of ten Arab countries, most of whom have been absorbed by Israel (See Appendix 26–Jewish Population in Arab countries), in effect a population exchange took place.

While the Jewish refugees from the Arab/Muslim lands have been integrated into Israeli society, the Arab refugees have been made pariahs within Arab states. They have been kept in perpetual refugee status, passed on from generation to generation, to act as in the words of Egyptian President Gamal Abdel Nasser: "A demographic bomb" against the Jewish state. They have become the recipients of never-ending funding by the outside world, mainly by United States taxpayers (directly or through the United Nations) and the European Union. Until 1973 Israel donated more to the United Nations Relief and Works Agency for Palestine Refugees in the Near East (UNRWA), than any Arab state. Even by the mid-1990s, Israel's contribution was larger than any Arab state except for Saudi Arabia, Kuwait, and Morocco.

TABLE 1

ANNUAL CONTRIBUTIONS TO UNRWA (2000)	
Grand total $293,207,000	
DONOR	**PERCENTAGE**
United States	31.57
European Community	18.53
United Kingdom	9.74
Netherlands	7.86
Sweden	6.54
Norway	4.50
Canada	3.80
Saudi Arabia, Kuwait, other Gulf Emirates	2.19
35 other countries	15.27

Source: http://info.jpost.com/C003/Supplements/Refugees/6-7.html and http://politicalmavens.com/index.php/2008/04/27/4560/?print=1

Much of that funding has not gone to the Arab people, but rather to their leadership and ends up in Swiss and Cayman Island bank accounts. It is used to purchase weapons and munitions to carry on their war against Israel. To enhance this perpetual status, while all the world's refugee problems are handled by the United Nations High Commissioner for Refugees (UNHCR), the Palestinian Arabs have an entire United Nations agency–United Nations Relief and Works Agency for Palestine Refugees in the Near East (UNRWA) assigned to them, with a bloated bureaucracy of 25,000 employees, to "assist" them.

9. If one accepts the Arab/Muslim argument that Israeli communities–towns and villages–are "occupied settlements," then one accepts the premise that Israel should not exist at all.

The Arab/Muslim world's war against the Jewish people predates the reestablishment of Jewish sovereignty over the ancient Jewish homeland as the State of Israel in 1948. The first Jewish victim of Arab terrorism, killed January 1, 1873, was Aharon Hershler, who is buried in the Jewish cemetery on the Mount of Olives in Jerusalem. The Arab/Muslim side views **ALL** Jewish cities, towns and villages as settlements on "occupied" land. This did not begin after the Six Day War of 1967 when Israel, in a defensive war, regained control of Judea, Samaria, the Golan Heights and Gaza. The Palestine Liberation Organization Covenant of 1964 declares that all of Israel is illegal and "occupied" Arab land (See Appendix 10–The Palestinian National Covenant, the Hamas Covenant, and Fatah Constitution).

Pre-1967 Jordanian maps, especially of Jerusalem, labels the land west of the Old City (then under Jordanian occupation) as "Occupied Territory of Palestine." The Hamas Charter, similarly declares that all of Israel, not just Judea, Samaria or Gaza, are "occupied" (See Appendix 13–The Arab [Jordanian] occupation of Jerusalem 1948-1967).

The Arabs and other Muslims claim the core of the Arab-Israel conflict is "occupation." That is true in Arab terminology where they consider all of Israel as "occupied." But it is not "occupation" but rather the Arab/Muslim preoccupation with destroying the Jewish state that is the core of the conflict. The issue has never been one of "occupation" but rather whether a Jewish state has the right to exist in the Middle East.

TRADITION/HISTORY

10. "Tradition says..." - is a powerful force in the Arab world.

Someone may reach for a gun if you "insult" their tradition. This is tied to their concept of "honor." View this as a cautionary warning–especially to first time visitors to the region.

11. In the Arab world, pride, dignity, and honor tend to outrank truth on any scale of political values.

Honor killings for example have been committed in the Arab Islamic world for over 1,400 years. Examples of this occurred on November 1, 2006, when Pakistani immigrant Mohammed Riaz burned his wife and four daughters (aged 3 to 16) to death because they had become too "Westernized.". Before the murders, he had destroyed "Western clothes" belonging to the girls. Most recently on December 9, 2007 another well publicized honor killing took place when a Canadian Muslim teenager, Aqsa Parvez was strangled, in Missauga, Toronto, Canada, and died the next day. Her father was arrested and charged with her murder. The girl's "offense" was trying to establish her own identity by moving out of her family home and for defying her father's command to cover her head with a *hijab*.

12. Throughout history there has been East-West rivalry and/or confrontation in the Middle East. The Land of Israel was invaded both from the southwest and from the northeast. The Gaza Strip was historically the invasion route from the southwest while the Jordan Valley was the northeastern route.

It is not necessarily an asset to be located at the crossroads of three continents where invaders can and have attacked. To survive a nation needs a strong military. The first major invasion on record was the Egyptian invasion at the end of King Solomon's reign, 928 BCE. The Assyrian invasion in 725 resulted in the fall of Samaria in 722 and the disappearance of the Northern Kingdom of Israel. The Chaldean (New Babylonian) invasions in 598 and 588 resulted in the destruction of Jerusalem and of the First Temple in 586, and there were quite a few additional invasions in between. The geopolitics has not changed over the last 3,000 years.

13. The history of the Arab/Muslim world starts in 622 CE; anything that happened before that is an irrelevant myth.

Consequently, the Muslims do not recognize world history before 622, including the history of the Jewish nation which continued for some 2,000 years before 622 CE. However, the Arab claim that the country they call "Palestine" was theirs and was taken away from them by the Jews is completely false and lacks any historic basis.

Israel became a nation in c. 1300 BCE, i.e. 2,000 years before the rise of Islam, and long before there was any Arab nation. Israel has been the homeland of the Jewish people since biblical times. It was subsequently "occupied" more than 15 times. Among its occupiers were the Egyptians, the Assyrians, the Chaldeans (New Babylonians), the Persians, the Greeks, the Romans, the Byzantines, the Arabs, the Seljuks, the Crusaders, the Ayyubids, the Mamelukes, and the Ottoman Turks. The longest occupiers of the Land of Israel, who ruled for 400 years between 1517 and 1917, were the Ottoman Turks. They were followed by the British who ruled under a Mandate of the League of Nations which later passed to the United Nations to endorse the homeland for the Jewish people.

Jews had dominion over the Land of Israel over 1,300 years before their expulsion by the conquering Romans. Moreover, Jews have had a continuous presence in this land over 3,300 years.

One may recall the prophecy of the Prophet Joel: *"For behold, in those days and in that time, when I shall bring again the captivity of Judah and Jerusalem, I will also gather all nations and will bring them down to the valley of Jehoshaphat, and will plead with them there for My people and for My heritage, Israel, whom they have scattered among the nations, and parted my land."* (Joel 4:1-2 in the Sinai Edition of the Tanach)

14. Throughout history, Islam sought to conquer the West and destroy its civilization.

According to Islam, the world is divided into two parts: ***Dar al-Islam***–House of submission and ***Dar al-Harb***—House of War. ***Dar al-Islam*** refers to those lands under Islamic rule, while ***Dar al-Harb*** refers to those areas outside Muslim rule; those lands administered by non-Muslim government. Any act of war or violence against the Dar al-Harb is morally justified. Hence Arab/Muslim states do not denounce as terrorism any act perpetrated against Jewish Israel,

Hindu India, Orthodox Serbia or Russia, Catholic Philippines, and Buddhist Thailand to cite but a few examples.

The first concerted effort to conquer the West, i.e. Europe, occurred in the 7th and 8th centuries. After sweeping out of the Arabian Peninsula, they conquered North Africa, and crossed the water straights dominated by the mountain that still bears the name of the Arab conqueror, Tariq ibn Ziyad, the mountain of Tariq (Jebel Tariq = Gibraltar). Then they overran the entire Iberian Peninsula. The Muslim hordes were stopped by Charles Martel at the Battle of Poitiers, near Tours, France in 732 CE.

The second attempt came during the 14th-17th centuries, as the Muslim forces of Ottoman Turkey sought to conquer Europe, this time from the east. On September 11-12, 1683, a combined Polish-Austrian-German force led by Jan III Sobieski, the King of Poland, demolished the Islamic army of Turks and Tartars at the gates of Vienna, Austria. The Battle of Vienna marked the high water mark of militant Islam's efforts to subjugate Europe a second time.

The third attempt began in the 1970s, with the spread of militant Sunni Wahhabist ideology from Saudi Arabia, and after 1979, the spread of similar militant Islam, Shiite in eschatology, from Iran. This time the goal is not merely the subjugation of Europe, but of the entire world. That battle is still on-going globally from the Philippines, through Thailand, India, Afghanistan, Iraq, Chechnya, Somalia, Israel, Kosovo, Algeria, and in cities scattered across Europe and the United States (See Appendix 11–The Spread of Islam).

Because the third spread of Islam is not focused like the first two were, today's Islamofascists must be defeated worldwide piecemeal, rather than in a single decisive battle. (See Appendix 12–Time line of Islam, Muslim conquests and setbacks).

15. Arab/Muslim conquerors have a penchant for destroying other people's religious shrines and building their own on the ruins. It was (and remains) Islam's way of saying, "We have defeated you, we rule you, and our god–Allah– is greater than your god."

Some prominent examples are:

- Islam's holiest shrine–the Kabba in Mecca–is an older pagan shrine.
- The construction of Ibrahimi Mosque over the Cave of the Biblical Patriarchs—Abraham, Isaac, and Jacob—in Hebron in 637.
- The Dome of the Rock was constructed on the ruins of the Jewish Temple Mount in Jerusalem, in 691.
- Al Aqsa Mosque was built at the southern end of the Temple Mount and also over the Basilica of St. Mary in 712.
- The Grand Mosque of Damascus, was built over the Cathedral of St. John the Baptist in 715.
- In India, the Hindu Vikramasli temple was razed to the ground in the 13th century, and its foundation stones thrown into the Ganges.
- Hagia Sophia in Istanbul, Turkey. It had been a Byzantine cathedral, the largest in the world, for nearly one thousand years. It had been built between 532 and 537 on the orders of the Byzantine Emperor Justinian. In 1453, Istanbul (then Constantinople) was conquered by the Muslim Ottoman

Turks, and Sultan Mehmed II ordered the building to be converted into a mosque. Only in 1935, was it converted into a museum by the secular Republic of Turkey. With the current government of Turkey moving steadily towards establishing an Islamic Republic, Hagia Sophia will probably be restored as a mosque.

- The Babri Mosque constructed by order of the first Mughal emperor of India, Babur, in Ayodhya in 1527. Babur's commander-in-chief Mir Baki destroyed an existing temple at the site, the Hindu temple that commemorated the birthplace of Rama, an incarnation of Vishnu, and ruler of Ayodhya, India. In a rare instance of a population trying to return the holy site to its original religious importance, a crowd of over 150,000 attacked and destroyed the Babri Mosque on December 6, 1992.

- Sultan Ahmed I, built in 1609, the Blue Mosque on the site of the Great Palace of the Byzantine Christian emperor.

- The Jewish Quarter in the Old City in Jerusalem was destroyed in 1948-1949. Numerous synagogues and religious schools of learning, including the famous Ramban synagogue constructed in 1267, were obliterated (See Appendix 13–The Arab [Jordanian] occupation of Jerusalem 1948-1967).

- On November 26, 1970, the Cathedral of the Sacred Heart in Tripoli, Libya, was converted into the Gamal Abdel Nasser Mosque.

- In September 1996, Palestinian Arabs desecrated and destroyed the Biblical Patriarch Joseph's Tomb, in Shchem (Nablus) including a synagogue. Then, in October 2000, the reconstructed synagogue and yeshiva at Joseph's Tomb was sacked and burned by Arab mobs, and Rabbi Hillel

Lieberman, who went there hoping to save Torah scrolls and other holy objects, was murdered. The next day his bullet-ridden body was found in a cave. On October 10, 2003, Arab mobs destroyed the site again and the Jewish holy site is buried under the new mosque that was built over the ruins of Joseph's Tomb.

- In Kosovo in 1999, more than 100 ancient Orthodox holy places were destroyed, some dating back to the 13th through 15th centuries.
- Two 1,400 year-old Buddha statues in the Bamiyan Valley of Afghanistan, were blown up in March 2001. This came after a *fatwa* (a religious edict), ordered by the Taliban, directed that all Afghan "idols" be destroyed as anti-Muslim.
- The Arab Muslims have attempted to appropriate the tomb of Rabbi Ashi, near Kibbutz Menara, in northern Israel. Rabbi Ashi, who died in 427, was a celebrated Jewish religious scholar, and the first editor of the Babylonian Talmud. The Shiite Muslims claim the tomb is not that of Rabbi Ashi, but rather of a Shiite leader in Lebanon who died in the 17th century. As a result of the Israeli withdrawal from southern Lebanon in May 2000, and the United Nations drawing the international boundary line, the border fence runs through the tomb!
- In 1996 the Arab Muslims constructed a new massive mosque adjacent to the Temple Mount in the area known as Solomon's Stables near the Eastern Hulda Gate in Jerusalem. In 1997, the Western Hulda Gate passageway was converted into another mosque. In November 1999, a buried Crusader-era door was reopened as an "emergency exit" for the mosque located within the Solomon's Stables area, opening an

excavation 18,000 square feet in size and up to 36 feet deep. In early 2001, Arab bulldozers continued their destruction including an ancient arched structure located adjacent to the eastern wall of the Temple Mount. Some 6,000 square meters of the Temple Mount were dug up, paved, and declared to be open air mosques. Some of the earth and rubble removed was dumped in the El-Azaria and in the Kidron Valleys. There was virtually no archaeological supervision over this digging.

- Without any real protest and action by the world in general and the Israeli government in particular, the Islamization of the entire Temple Mount continued. In July 2007, the Waqf Muslim religious trust began digging a ditch from the northern side of the Temple Mount compound to the Dome of the Rock as a prelude to what was termed "infrastructure work." The vandalism, desecration and destruction of Jewish antiquities on the Temple Mount continue. All this construction in 1996, 1997, 1999, 2001, and 2007 has been a deliberate, calculated attempt to destroy the physical evidence of the Jewish claim to the Temple Mount.

- Currently there is an Arab/Muslim attempt to deny the Jewish connection to the Biblical matriarch Rachel's Tomb, located just south of Jerusalem on the northern approaches to Bethlehem. The Arabs claim that the enclosure is a mosque, Bilal Bin Rabbah, and there have been numerous attempted attacks on Rachel's Tomb. The Israeli government has had to build security barriers on three sides of the site. Access is now restricted to pilgrims and tourists approaching from Israel.

16. Throughout the history of the modern Middle East, the Arabs have claimed to be "victims" entitled to compensation–acquiescence to their maximal demands.

They claim they were the victims of Ottoman Turkish domination, British and French colonization, United States imperialism, Israeli "occupation," (See Appendix 14–Some Historic Occupations) and repression by autocratic and dictatorial Arab regimes.

This claim has developed into the veritable cottage industry of perpetual "victim hood." They use this sense of "victim hood" to justify the murder and mayhem perpetrated against the West in general and Israel in particular. Lately, a religious element has been added calling for *jihad* against the infidels–the Christians, Jews, Bahá'ís, Hindus, Buddhists, animists, and others. *Jihad* is a communal and religious duty of Muslims against the ***harbi***–the non-believers.

17. There has been a continual and massive Palestinian/Arab policy of role reversal and transmutation.

Among the myths being foisted on the world are:

- Jesus was a "Palestinian," not a Judean.
- Jesus was a Muslim prophet not a Jewish sage or the Christian Savior.
- The population of the Palestinian Arabs is always greater than the population of Israel.
- The Palestinian Arabs speak of their "tragedy" as the Holocaust, denying the Holocaust perpetrated on the Jews, 1939-1945.
- Israel took over Palestine, displacing its original inhabitants.

- The Arabs were driven into the desert whereas Arab leaders have vowed to drive the Jews into the sea. This vow reached a crescendo in May-June 1967.
- The Palestinian covenant replaces the Biblical covenant between God and the Jewish people.
- The Palestinian Arabs claim a **_Haq al-Auda_** (right of return) to replace the Israeli Law of Return whereby any Jew may return to Israel and become a citizen.
- The Israelis are doing to the Arabs what the Nazis did to the Jews (presumably killing them by the millions in gas chambers).

ISLAM

18. The ideology of Islam is based on the Qur'an, which is considered Allah's literal word. This has been followed and practiced for 1,400 years. According to Islam, the world is divided into Dar al-Islam (House of submission) and Dar al-Harb (the House of war). Islamic ideology calls for three choices to be given to non-believers, convert, submit to a subordinate status (dhimmitude) (See Appendix 15–Dhimmi status) and pay jizya (per capita tax tribute–or face war and death.

This supremacist ideology is based on the "immutable" words of Allah as recorded in the **Qur'an**. The **Qur'an** contains 114 *suras* (chapters). The first 87 *suras* are known as the "Meccan" *suras*–the revelation purportedly received by Muhammad via the messenger/angel Gabriel. These *suras* are widely regarded by experts on Islamic scripture as being the more benign revelations that Muhammad received. The following 27 *suras* were "revealed" to Muhammad following his migration to Yathrib (Medina). The Medinan *suras* are widely regarded by experts on Islamic scripture as being much more belligerent, violent and supremacist than the "Meccan" *suras*. It was in Medina, that Muhammad became a warlord. More importantly, the latter "Medinan" *suras* which were revealed to Muhammad are regarded and upheld as being MORE AUTHORITATIVE than the former *suras* which were revealed to him.

- *Fight against them until idolatry is no more and God's religion reigns supreme. (2:193)*
- *The [only] religion [acceptable] before God is Islam. (3:19)*
- *If anyone desires a religion other than Islam, never will it be accepted of him. (3: 85)*
- *You are the noblest community ever raised up for mankind. (3:110)*
- *We will put terror into the hearts of the unbelievers. (3:150)*
- *Men have authority over women because God has made the one superior to the other,... Good women are obedient. As for those from whom you fear disobedience, admonish them, forsake them in beds apart, and beat them." (4:34)*
- *The true believers fight for the cause of God, but the infidels fight for the devil. Fight then against the friends of Satan. (4:76)*
- *The unbelievers are your inveterate enemy. (4:101)*
- *Believers, take neither the Jews nor the Christians for your friends. (5:51)*
- *I shall cast terror into the hearts of the infidels. Strike off their heads; strike off the very tips of their fingers. (8:12)* ▲
- *Fight them until all opposition ends and all submit to Allah. So fight them until there is no more Fitnah (disbelief [non-Muslims]) and all submit to the religion of Allah alone (in the whole world). (8:39)*
- *Make war on them [non-Muslims] until idolatry shall cease and God's religion shall reign supreme. (8:40)*

- *Surely the vilest of animals in Allah's sight are those who disbelieve. (8:55)*
- *Fight and kill the disbelievers wherever you find them, take them captive, harass them, lie in wait and ambush them using every stratagem of war.(9:5)*
- *Fight those who do not believe until they all surrender, paying the protective tax in submission. (9:29)*
- *Prophet, make war on the unbelievers and the hypocrites and deal rigorously with them. (9:73 and 66:9)*
- *Allah has purchased from the faithful their lives and worldly goods, and in return has promised them Paradise. They will fight for the cause of Allah; they will slay and be slain. (9:111)*
- *Believers, make war on the infidels who dwell around you. Deal firmly with them. (9:123)*
- *When you meet the unbelievers in the battlefield, strike off their heads. (47:4)* ▲
- *The unbelievers among the people of the book and the pagans shall burn forever in the fire of Hell. They are the vilest of all creatures. (98:6).*

▲ These two **suras** bring to mind the beheadings of Daniel Pearl, reporter for the *Wall Street Journal* on February 1, 2002, and American businessman Nicholas Berg on May 7, 2004. The public was horrified when videotapes of both executions were broadcast globally. Most recently, on January 19, 2008, Hezbollah leader Sheikh Hassan Nasrallah stated that his armed group had body parts of Israeli soldiers killed in Lebanon during the 2006 conflict. He said they had the *"heads, the hands, the feet and even a nearly intact cadaver from the head down to the pelvis."*

Over a century ago, former US Consul to Ottoman-controlled Palestine (1893-1898), Edwin Sherman Wallace provided this seemingly timeless insight regarding Muslims, written in 1908, almost a decade prior to the Balfour Declaration:

"Their religion [Islam] is intolerant. It has little sympathy for the adherents of other faiths. It once advocated an extermination of the infidels. Perhaps it would continue in that advocacy did its leaders dare."– As related in his memoirs "Jerusalem the Holy," New York, 1908, p. 344.

Any call for "reform" or "moderation" of radical Islamic ideology must overcome 1,400 years of Islamic tradition and religious scholarship, which consider any attempt to reinterpret the *Qur'an* as heresy, punishable by death.

19. All Muslim religious scholars and authorities consider that Islam is a "complete way of life."

You can find this phrase on all Muslim websites including the Council of American-Islamic Relations (CAIR). Most non-Muslims have no idea what this really means. Yet, this characteristic of Islam is extremely important because 1) it affects the unwillingness of Muslim immigrants in our country to assimilate, and 2) Muslims, according to Islamic law, are required to strive to impose this "complete way of life" on everybody in the world.

For example: Muslim **Sharia** (Islamic law) tells people how to dress, what kind of pictures they can have in their homes, how to use the toilet, what they can eat and when, who can marry whom, who they are allowed to befriend, and who they must fight and subdue.

Traditional Sharia (Islamic law) has been supported by all the Islamic scholars and religious authorities for 1,400 years.

20. Muslim women and children are dispensable. Infidel women and children are prime targets for rape, slavery and genocide.

Religious and sexual apartheid are practiced in Arab/Muslim countries.

The status of women can be summarized as follows:

TABLE 2
Status of Women under
***Sharia* (Islamic Law)**

	UNDER SHARIA (Islamic law)
Society	Needs of the community are paramount; patriarchal society based on gender apartheid with women reduced to a lowly state of fear; no opportunity for individual freedom and equality.
Dress	Forced to wear the hijab (a hair-covering); a jilbab (a garment that leaves only the face and hands exposed); a niqab (a total covering except for the eyes) or the burqa (a total head and body covering).
Sexuality	Many Muslim girls are victims of female genital mutilation; there is female sexual and domestic slavery.

Marriage	Basic love, and being in love is forbidden; Polygamy is the rule rather than the exception; In Saudi Arabia women are forbidden to date; In Iran, enclaves in Iraq, and Hezbollah-controlled sections of Lebanon, high school girls are forbidden to hold hands with boy friends; marriage–in some countries as young as nine and arranged marriages are often to men much, much older; women do not sign their own marriage certificate.
Assault	Women and daughters are routinely beaten for even minor offenses; if raped women are most often punished, the rapist is not.
Divorce	Husband may invoke *talaq* saying "I divorce you" three times to be divorced. Divorce is forbidden to women; Women thus divorced receive no support and usually lose custody of children.
Family	Muslims are to have more children to increase the umma–the community of Muslims; a son's inheritance should be twice the size of that of a daughter.
Travel	No leaving the house without a male relative; in Saudi Arabia women are forbidden to drive a car.
Education and Economic independence	No schooling; Cannot go out of the house to work; economic and social dependence on men.
Political rights	The Qur'an declares that a woman's testimony is worth half that of a man; In many Muslim nations, e.g. Saudi Arabia, women can't vote.

NOTE: When the Taliban controlled Afghanistan, in addition to the above mentioned restrictions, chatting with the other gender was a crime; movies, mixed schools, radios, dish antennas, music and poetry were banned. If the Islamofascists win the global conflict and re-establish the Caliphate, that will be the society they would establish.

21. Suicide is a sin in Islam except when done to kill infidels, when it becomes a virtue rewarded in Paradise, with 72 virgins.

This is exemplified by **Sura 9:111** in the **Qur'an**, which states (several translations follow):

YUSUF ALI: *Allah hath purchased of the believers their persons and their goods; for theirs (in return) is the garden (of Paradise): they fight in His cause, and slay and are slain: a promise binding on Him in truth, through the Law, the Gospel, and the Qur'an: and who is more faithful to his covenant than Allah? Then rejoice in the bargain which ye have concluded: that is the achievement supreme.*

PICKTHAL: *Lo! Allah hath bought from the believers their lives and their wealth because the Garden will be theirs: they shall fight in the way of Allah and shall slay and be slain. It is a promise which is binding on Him in the Torah and the Gospel and the Qur'an. Who fulfilleth His covenant better than Allah? Rejoice then in your bargain that ye have made, for that is the supreme triumph.*

SHAKIR: *Surely Allah has bought of the believers their persons and their property for this, that they shall have the garden; they fight in Allah's way, so they slay and are slain; a promise which is binding on Him in the Taurat and the Injeel and the Qur'an; and who is more faithful to his covenant than Allah? Rejoice therefore in the pledge which you have made; and that is the mighty achievement.*

This martyrdom verse is taken to mean that the slain martyr need not wait until Judgment Day in order to get his virgins in Paradise. He goes straight to Paradise.

There are scholars who believe that the date of the attacks on the United States by Osama Bin Laden's Al Qaeda on September 11, 2001–i.e. "9-11" was inspired by this verse.

POLITICS

22. In the Middle East disputed areas are known by different names for the same geographical place - strictly for political motives.

Examples of this include:
- Hatay = Livaa aliskenderna
- Western Sahara = southern Morocco
- Persian Gulf = Arabian Gulf
- Khuzistan = Arabistan
- Gulf of Eilat = Gulf of Aqaba
- Mount Dov = Shebaa Farms
- Jerusalem = Al Quds
- Shchem = Nablus
- Eilat = Umm Rashrash
- Hebron = Al Khalil
- Israel = "Palestine"
- Judea and Samaria = the "West Bank"
- The Temple Mount = Haram esh-Sharif, or Noble Sanctuary

23. Elections do not make a Middle East democracy

The victory of Hamas in the Palestinian Legislative elections of January 25, 2006, has been cited by its supporters both in the Middle East and abroad as proof that "the people have spoken through the democratic process" and the world should now sit down and negotiate with this gang of religiously motivated killers. Furthermore extremist Islamist groups such as the Muslim Brotherhood gained seats in the

Egyptian parliament and enabled Hezbollah to gain a share of power in Lebanon. Elections do not make a democracy.

First it must be noted that although Hamas gained 44% of the popular vote, it was given 74 seats in the 132-seat legislature–56% of the seats. Fatah, which placed second with 42% of the popular vote was given 45 seats, which amounted to only 34% of the seats!

Adolf Hitler's victory in the "democratic" German election of 1932, which along with those held by such other "democratic election" stalwarts (I am being facetious here) as Joseph Stalin, Mao Zedong, Gamal Abdel Nasser, Hafez al Assad and his son, Bashir; Saddam Hussein, and Muammar Qadhafi, to name but a few of many such despots, are examples of the proponents of tyranny and despotism using one element of the democratic system to gain power and then to destroy that very system.

Then Egyptian Premier Gamal Abdel Nasser staged a plebiscite on January 24, 1954 to ratify a new Egyptian constitution. The population of Egypt at the time was some 22,000,000. Of that number 5,697,467 registered to vote and 5,488,225 or 99.8% voted in favor, while 10,045 voted "no." At the same time Premier Nasser was elected president of Egypt by a greater majority 5,496,965 or 99.9% of the vote was in favor of him. Noteworthy of this election was despite the large numbers, only 150,000 women voted. Did this election make Egypt a democracy? The answer, which still applies today, is definitely not.

On March 29-30, 1979, the Iranian people were offered a simple yes or no vote referendum on creating an Islamic Republic. The result was 98.2% voted yes, while only 1.8% voted no. The Islamic Republic was established and democracy perished shortly thereafter.

In December 1991 elections were held for the 430-seat Algerian National Assembly. In the first round of voting the Islamic Salvation Front (FIS), won 231 seats with 50% or more of the votes. This would have led to a FIS victory, which was almost certain to win more than the 2/3 majority of seats required to change the Algerian Constitution. That would have enabled the FIS to impose an Islamic fundamentalist state and end democracy in largely secular Algeria. The immediate response was a military coup which cancelled the second round of voting. These events triggered the Algerian Civil War, which lasted from 1991 to 2002 at a cost of between 150,000 and 200,000 lives. The illustrative examples of Egypt, Iran, and Algeria all re-affirm the premise that an election does not make a democracy.

It is to be recalled that true, real democratization requires more than plebiscites. It is an evolutionary process towards constitutional government which entails the acceptance of human rights guarantees, liberal democratic values, freedom of expression, equality for women, an independent judiciary, institutional checks and balances, toleration of ethnic and religious minorities, and the desire to live at peace with other nations, among other factors. True democracies that consist of the features and values described above are not created by elections alone.

Adherents of true democracy know this fact. Real democracy is a painstakingly S-L-O-W process, especially when introduced to a region that never experienced it, but has been exposed to its influence from abroad and are desirous of it (like Eastern Europe under Soviet control and those who never experienced true democracy and whose people have been brainwashed by their religion against it (as in the case of the Arab/Muslim Middle East).

The Arab/Muslim world needs exposure to this true democracy and then to calls for change from within, not imposed from the outside. This will take time, there are no quick fixes. It will take decades, perhaps longer.

24. The political power that dominates the Nile has been and is the rival of the political power that controls the Tigris-Euphrates.

Table 3 illustrates historic examples and the validity of the statement.

TABLE 3
Nile River vs. Tigris-Euphrates Rivers rivalry

ERA	NILE POWER	TIGRIS-EUPHRATES POWER
20th-16th centuries BCE	Egypt*	Babylonia
6th century BCE	Egypt*	Assyria
590 BCE	Egypt*	Chaldean Empire
520 BCE	Egypt*	Persian Empire
192 BCE	Ptolemaic Kingdom	Seleucid Kingdom
1st century BCE – 2nd century CE	Roman Empire	Parthian Empire
12th century	Fatimid Empire	Ayyubid Empire
1805	Mohammad Ali	Ottoman Turkey

1882-1918	Great Britain	Ottoman Turkey
1945-1954	Egypt under King Farouk	Iraq under Nuri as-Said
1954-1990s	Egypt under Nasser, Sadat, and Mubarak	Iraq under Abdel Karim Qasim and Saddam Hussein

* See Appendix 16–Famous Kings, Queens and Pharaohs of Egypt.

25. The goal of Pan-Arab unity has proven to be largely illusory, like a mirage in the desert.

Through much of the last half of the 20th century, there have been numerous attempts at Pan-Arab unity–*al wahdah al arabiya*–made by various Arab states. A review of these attempts is in order:

TABLE 4
Attempts at Pan-Arab unity

DATE	NATIONS INVOLVED	OUTCOME
February 1, 1958	Egypt and Syria formed *The United Arab Republic*	Syria seceded, September 28, 1961
February 14, 1958	Iraq and Jordan formed *The Arab Federation*	Iraq withdrew, July 15, 1958
March 8, 1958	Egypt, Syria and Yemen formed *The United Arab States*	Syria seceded, September 28, 1961; Egypt terminated, December 26. 1961

February 11, 1959	Audhali, Beihan, Dhala, Fadhli, Lower Yafa, and Upper Aulaqi Sheikhdom formed *The Federation of Arab Emirates of the South*	British-sponsored federation; succeeded by the *Federation of South Arabia*
April 4, 1962	Federation of Arab Emirates of the South and Alawi, Aqrabi, Dathina, Haushabi, Lahej, Lower Aulaqi, Maflahi, Shaib, Wahidi (Wahidi Balhaf) joined to form *The Federation of South Arabia* Aden joined January 18, 1963 Upper Aulaqi Sultanate joined June 1964	British-sponsored federation opposed by nationalist forces. Federation abolished with the independence of the People's Republic of South Yemen on November 30, 1967
April 17, 1963	Egypt, Syria, and Iraq formed *The United Arab Republic*	Egypt repudiated, July 22, 1963
September 2, 1963	Syria and Iraq	Aborted
May 26, 1964	Egypt and Iraq	Aborted
July 13, 1964	Egypt and Yemen Arab Republic	Aborted
November 8, 1970	Egypt, Syria, Libya, and Sudan	Aborted

April 19, 1971	Egypt, Syria, and Libya formed *The Federation of Arab Republics*	Egypt abrogated, October 3, 1984
December 2, 1971	Abu Dhabi, Ajman, Dubai, Fujaira, Sharja, and Umm al-Qaiwain formed *The United Arab Emirates* Ras al-Khaima joined February 11, 1972	
August 2, 1972	Egypt and Libya	Aborted
November 28, 1972	Yemen Arab Republic and People's Democratic Republic of (South) Yemen	Aborted
January 12, 1974	Libya and Tunisia formed *The Arab Islamic Republic*	Tunisia repudiated, January 15, 1974
December 8, 1976	Syria and Jordan	Aborted
December 21, 1976	Egypt and Syria	Aborted
January 28, 1979	Syria and Iraq	Aborted
March 30, 1979	Yemen Arab Republic and People's Democratic Republic of (South) Yemen	Aborted
September 10, 1980	Libya and Syria	Aborted
January 6, 1981	Libya and Chad	Aborted

August 14, 1984	Libya and Morocco formed *The Arab-African Federation*	Morocco repudiated, August 29, 1986
October 1988	Libya and Sudan	Aborted
February 17, 1989	Libya, Yemen Arab Republic, People's Democratic Republic of (South) Yemen, Oman, and Djibouti were to form an *Arab Sahel State*	Proposed by Libya but not acted upon
May 23, 1990	Yemen Arab Republic, and People's Democratic Republic of (South) Yemen formed *The Republic of Yemen*	Rebel PDRY forces attempted to secede May 21, 1994. They were defeated in a short, but furious civil war that ended July 10, 1990.

One of the most important underlying developments in the Arab world is that states, a relatively new and awkward idea in the region's long history, have put down roots and developed specific identities. Despite the fact the many of the Arab states were creations of British, French, and Italian colonial powers with arbitrarily-drawn borders, a sense of nationalism grew within these states. That nationalism has proven stronger than the drive towards Pan-Arab unity. A prime example was Iraq in 1958. The violent and bloody coup that removed the Hashemite monarchy of King Feisal II was largely instigated, encouraged and supported by the United Arab Republic's President Gamal Abdel Nasser. Nasser's expectation was that Iraq would immediately join the UAR. This would bring added territory, prestige and most importantly, oil-revenues to the new unified Arab state. However, Iraqi strongman Abdel Karim Qasim quickly realized that merger into the UAR would at best bring him a regional governorship, whereas staying a separate independent nation would bring him all the power and perks of a national head of state. Iraq thus never joined the UAR. The concept of one Arab nation has proven elusive, constantly coming into conflict with state interests.

Thus all attempts at Arab unity failed, with the exception of the establishment of the United Arab Emirates and the Republic of Yemen. In the case of the former there was high motivation to succeed as each emirate was tiny in size and relatively weak. The union was fostered by the concept of strength in numbers. In the case of the Republic of Yemen it was more an issue of obliterating an artificially drawn British colonial boundary line and reuniting a historic nation, though there too unification has been marred by the civil war of 1993.

The old ideologies from Nasserism to Arab Socialism to Ba'athism have proven to be bankrupt and incapable of solving the fundamental political, economic and social problems of Arab societies. Some Arabs have begun to comprehend that Arab unity was a utopian dream that was incompatible with their reality. This has produced cynicism and a sense of impotence and that in turn has created a wide opening for frustration. There is an ideological vacuum, a feeling that all the political solutions have been tried and none of them have worked. That void is now being filled by a *jihadist* religious fundamentalism which offers a messianic solution that secular politics has failed to deliver. Thus as pan-Arabism declined, pan-Islamism rose in its place.

ALLIANCES

26. The maxim: "The enemy of my enemy is my friend" applies, with the notable exceptions of Sunnis vs. Shiites and Arabs vs. Iran where the converse of the maxim is true: "The enemy of your enemy is not necessarily your friend."

A prime example of this maxim was the French-Israeli alliance in 1954. At that time France was combating Arab rebels in Algeria, aided by Egypt's President Gamal Abdel Nasser, who was also the mortal enemy of Israel. Hence France and Israel drew closer together, to deal with the common enemy culminating in the Sinai-Suez War of 1956.

The converse is true of Saudi Arabia and Iraq. Both were opponents of growing Shiite influence emanating from Iran. While Israel has been an enemy of Iran, it does not follow that Israel is the friend of either Saudi Arabia or Iraq.

27. Turkey usually allies itself with whichever great power opposes Russia.

In modern times Turkey has fought the Russians fourteen times in 1568-69, 1678-81, 1695-1700, 1710-1711, 1722-1724, 1736-1739,

1768-1774, 1787-1792, 1806-1812, 1827 (During the Greek War of Independence), 1828-1829, 1853-1856 (The Crimean War), 1877-1878, and 1914-1918 (World War I). This helps explain why Turkey became part of the North Atlantic Treaty Organization (NATO) alliance in 1952, during the Cold War (1945-1991).

WAR

28. *In the Middle East weakness guarantees aggression.*

- During World War I, the perception as well as the fact that Ottoman Turkey was weak–the "sick man" of Europe,– encouraged the Great Arab Revolt of 1916 led by the Hashemites.
- The perception of weakness and the policy of appeasement by Great Britain over crises in Ethiopia, Spain and later the Sudetenland, encouraged the Arab Revolt of 1936-1939 in Mandatory Palestine.
- The apparent weakness of Great Britain desperately trying to survive the Nazi onslaught in 1940-1941, encouraged the pro-Axis coup in Iraq led by Rashid al-Gailani.
- The apparent weakness of the Yishuv (Jewish community) in Mandatory Palestine, numbering just 650,000 people, bereft of assistance from any quarter, encouraged the Arab aggression of 1947-1949 against the nascent Jewish state, which was attacked by the combined military forces of seven Arab nations counting 37.4 millions.

- The perception that Israel in the spring of 1967 was weak, a "spoiled espresso generation" influenced Egyptian President Gamal Abdel Nasser to rapidly move towards confrontation with Israel.
- The weakness of Lebanon, wracked by civil war in 1975 encouraged Syria to intervene and then occupy Lebanon for 29 years from 1976 to 2005.
- The Iraqi attack on Iran in September 1980 was in part calculated upon Iran's perceived weakness after the Iranian Revolution of the preceding year.
- The Iraqi invasion and occupation of Kuwait in 1990 was based in part on the weakness of the U.S. commitment to Kuwait.
- The Hamas and Hezbollah attacks on Israel in June-July 2006 was due to the perception of Israeli weakness manifested in the unilateral Israeli withdrawal from southern Lebanon in May 2000, and from Gaza and northern Samaria in August 2005, uprooting of Jewish communities, as well as by the release of terrorist prisoners—"with blood on their hands"– all without any Israeli counter-demands.

29. *Constant talk of the "Israeli-Palestinian conflict" is based on a false premise that makes it seem smaller in the overall context of the Middle East. It better serves Arab/Muslim propaganda efforts. The misnamed Palestinian Arabs are portrayed as a "tiny, impoverished, out-gunned, homeless people" fighting against the mighty Israeli military.*

In fact, it role reverses the historic reality of miniscule democratic Israel continually being attacked. The Arab-Israeli encounter has grown larger over the years. In 1947 when the Arab states rejected the UN Partition plan for Palestine, there were seven Arab League states, which engaged in a military attack to destroy the nascent Jewish state. It was truly a "Goliath vs. David" struggle with Israel as "David." Today, there are 21 sovereign Arab states, largely oil rich countries, (See Appendix 17–The League of Arab States) with a huge population and land mass. There are 22 if one counts the non-existent state of "Palestine" that is on the Arab League membership roster. To this must be added all the various terrorist organizations–Fatah, the Popular Front for the Liberation of Palestine, Islamic Jihad, Hamas, Hezbollah et al. Thus there is a much larger Arab "Goliath." Add to this the non-Arab Muslim states, including Iran, and Pakistan not to mention the 57 members of the Organization of the Islamic Conference, all of which have demonstrated open hostility to Israel.

30. The Arab/Muslim exaggerated emphasis on the "Palestinian-Israeli conflict" is over-emphasized to the point that it obscures the far worse conflicts, ethnic cleansing, murders, assassinations and destruction perpetrated within the Islamic world as well as jihadist attacks worldwide against the West.

To list the most prominent examples:

TABLE 5
Modern conflict in the Middle East (excluding the Arab-Israel conflict)

1915-1923	Turkish Muslim genocide against 1.5 million Christian Armenians, 750,000 Assyrians, and 400,000 Greeks.
1923 to date	Turkey-Iraq dispute.

1924 to date	Jordan-Saudi Arabia dispute over the claim of suzerainty maintained by the Hashemite dynasty of Jordan over the Saudi province of Hejaz, where the holy cities of Mecca and Medina are located.
1936-1974	Iran-Iraq fought a series of wars for control of the Shatt al-Arab border estuary.
1943 to date	Syria-Lebanon dispute. Syria has never recognized a separate independent Lebanon. Syria notoriously claims the entirety of Lebanon as part of "Greater Syria."
1945 to date	Iran-Afghanistan dispute over the waters of three border rivers.
1947	The partition of the Indian Subcontinent resulted in between 800,000-1,000,000 Muslims and Hindus killed.
1949	Insurrection suppressed in Lebanon.
1954-1962	French-Algerian National Liberation Front (FLN) conflict saw 675,000 mostly Muslims killed by both the French and the Muslim FLN. In addition, between 50,000 and 150,000 *harkis* (pro-French Muslim Algerians) were killed by the FLN.
1955	Saudi Arabia-Oman and Saudi Arabia-Abu Dhabi border clashes over Buraimi Oasis.
1955-1972	Civil War in the Sudan saw 500,000-600,000 mostly Christians and animists killed.
1958	Violent revolution in Iraq overthrew the Hashemite monarchy.
1958	Civil war in Lebanon and intervention by the United Arab Republic.
1958	Civil strife in Jordan and intervention by the United Arab Republic.
1959	Failed Nasserist coup in Iraq triggered a communist rampage, some 3,000 were killed.
1959	Iraqi communists attacked Turcoman population in Kirkuk, at least 500 killed.

1961 to date	Muslim Indonesian genocide against West Papuans has resulted in 100,000-400,000 killed.
1961-1970, 1973-1975, 1980-1991	Kurdish revolt in Iraq.
1962-1970	Civil War in Yemen and the 1962-1967 Egyptian intervention in Yemen; resulted in 100,000-150,000 killed. This included the use of poison gas–confirmed by the International Red Cross.
1962-1992	Civil war in Ethiopia, resulted in 1,400,000 Muslims and Christians killed.
1963-1964	Radafan uprising in Aden.
1963	14th of Ramadan Revolution in Iraq resulted in Ba'athists battling communists; some 1-5,000 were killed.
1963-1967	Nationalist uprising in Aden.
1963-1974	Greek-Turkish communal violence in Cyprus.
1964	Revolution in Zanzibar, resulted in some 17,000 killed, mostly Muslims.
1965-1966	During the attempted coup in Indonesia and its aftermath, some 500,000 Muslims were killed.
1965-1976	Separatist insurgency in Oman (Dhofar Province).
1968-2003	The Iraqi regime of Saddam Hussein engaged in the murderous repression and ethnic cleansing of the Kurdish people. This resulted in the deaths of over 200,000 to 300,000 killed–all Muslims. Over 1 million died during this period, the overwhelming majority Muslims.
1969, 1973	Saudi Arabia - P.D.R. (South)Yemen border clashes.
1969-1975	P.D.R. (South) Yemen-Oman border war, as Marxist rebels from the Popular Front for the Liberation of the Occupied Arab Gulf tried to seize control of the Omani province of Dhofar. That war claimed over 100,000 lives and produced almost a half-million refugees on both sides of the border.

1970	"Black September" saw 3,000-5,000 Jordanians and Palestinian Arabs killed in ten days.
1970-1971	Jordanian Civil War: Total deaths including "Black September" among Jordanians and Palestinian Arabs, all Muslims, were estimated at 25,000.
1970	Syrian invasion of Jordan.
1971	1,250,000 Muslims were killed during the Bangladesh secession from Pakistan and Bangladeshi War of Independence.
1972-1975	Iraq-Iran border clashes.
1972-1973, 1979, 1982	Yemen-P.D.R. (South)Yemen border clashes.
1973	Iraqi incursion and occupation of Kuwait.
1973	Sporadic uprisings by Kurds in Turkey.
1973-1975	Kurdish revolt in Iraq.
1974 to date	Turkish invasion and occupation of northern Cyprus.
1975-1991	Civil war in Lebanon. Over 130,000 dead. Over 500,000 Christians fled.
1975-1999	Muslim Indonesian genocide against Christians in Timor Este (East Timor) resulted in 200,000-300,000 killed.
1976-2005	Syrian intervention in and occupation of Lebanon.
1976 to date	Morocco-Algeria conflict over the status of the Western Sahara.
1977	Egypt-Libya border war.
1977 to date	Civil war, anarchy and nearly continual conflict in Somalia resulted in over 550,000 killed.
1978-1979	Revolution in Iran.
1979 to date	Iran-Pakistan dispute over territorial waters in the Arabian Sea.
1979	Islamic extremists occupy the Grand Mosque in Mecca, Saudi Arabia.

1979 to date	Iranian-Kurdish conflict has resulted in over 10,000 killed–all Muslims.
1980-1988	Iraq-Iran Gulf War I, resulted in between 1,000,000 and 1,600,000 Muslims killed on both sides.
1979-1999	Afghanistan civil war, resulting in some 2,400,000 Muslims killed.
1980-1981, 1983-1987	Libyan invasion and occupation of Chad. Thousands were killed.
1982	Muslim militant uprising and ruthless government suppression in Hama, Syria. Some 20,000 were killed.
1982-1984	U.S.-French-Italian peacekeeping forces in Lebanon, attacked, killed and forced to withdraw by Hezbollah terrorists.
1983	Palestine Liberation Organization civil war in Lebanon.
1983-2006	Civil War in the southern Sudan; some 1,900,000 killed.
1984	Kurdish revolt in Iran.
1984 to date	Turkish-Kurdish conflict has resulted in over 30,000 killed–all Muslims.
1986	Civil War in P.D.R. (South) Yemen.
1986-1989	Iraqi ethnic cleansing of the Kurds during the Al-Anfal campaign resulted in 50,000 to 182,000 killed.
1988	Iraqi government poison gas attack on Muslim Kurds in Halabja. Between 3,000 and 5,000 perish.
1988	Iranian government execution of over 5,000 "political prisoners" most of them Muslim.
1988	Iran began acting to ensure its hold over the oil-rich province of Khuzistan, the object of a pan-Arab campaign to claim the region as part of the "Arab homeland" since the 1970s. Ethnic cleansing of Arabs began.

1990 to date	Yemen-Oman boundary dispute.
1990-1991	Iraqi invasion, conquest and annexation of Kuwait. After Kuwait's liberation, nearly 400,000 Palestinians were expelled from Kuwait. In a like manner, Saudi Arabia expelled 800,000 Yemenis, due to Yemen's opposition to the liberation of Kuwait.
1991	Kurdish uprising in Iraq brutally suppressed by Iraqi regime.
1991-1992	The Shiite uprising in southern Iraq was brutally suppressed by the Iraqi government. Some 200,000 were killed–all Muslims.
1991-2002	Algerian Civil War. Between 150,000-200,000 were killed.
1992-1996	Civil war in Tajikistan with over 50,000 killed.
1992-1995	Bosnian war saw 102,622 dead, according to the 2004 research of the International Criminal Tribunal. At least, 63,994 were Muslims and of those some 38,000 were civilians.
1992-2002	More than 160,000 Muslims were killed in Algeria by Islamist terrorists.
1993	Civil war in Yemen.
1994-1996	The First Chechnya War, with an estimated 53,000-103,000, mainly Muslims, killed.
1994-1999	Yemen and Eritrea clashed over the Hanish Islands in the Red Sea.
1996 to date	Qatar-Saudi Arabia dispute over the oil-rich area of Khor al-Udaid.
1999 to date	The second Chechnya War, with 20,000 to 105,000, mainly Muslims, killed in the first four years.
1996-1999	War in Kosovo resulted in between 7,449-13,627 mostly Muslims killed, as well as the loss of over 1,000 Christian Serbs.

2001	Qatar-Bahrain naval war over control of the Hawar Islands.
2003	Egypt-Sudan border dispute over the Halaieb territory.
2003 to date	Insurgency terrorism by Ba'athist remnants of the former Iraqi regime assisted by foreign *jihadist* "volunteers" against the legitimate government of Iraq and U.S.-led coalition forces.
2003 to date	Sudanese Islamist government forces assisted by *janjaweed* militias perpetrated ethnic cleansing in Darfur; over 400,000 killed.
2005-2006	Chad-Sudan border war.
2005	Iraq's democratically elected parliament has yet to put aside Iraqi claims against the Kuwaiti islands of Warbah and Bubiyan as well as the southern portion of the Rumailah oilfields granted to Kuwait by the UN. The uncertainty has forced Kuwait to postpone its ambitious plans for developing Bubiyan into a free-trade zone; tourist projects in Warbah and in the nearby island of Failakah have also been frozen. To keep the Iraqis out, Kuwait has built a series of fortifications along the border, including electrified ditches, anti-tank traps, and a no-man's land at a depth of 10 miles.
2006	Saudi Arabia-Kuwait dispute over the 5,770 km² (2,228 sq. miles) "neutral zone."

It should be noted that no fewer than 43 conflicts over territory and resources, not one of them having anything to do with Israel and the Palestinian Arabs, have taken place in the greater Middle East in recent history.

These international disputes are quite apart from the uninterrupted string of domestic clashes, military coups, acts of sectarian and ethnic vengeance, factional terrorism, assassinations, and other internal conflicts that have characterized the region, attaining impressive heights of cruelty and despoliation.

With the exception of Israel the entire Middle East lacks a culture of conflict resolution, let alone the necessary mechanisms of meaningful compromise. It should be stressed that in the West, it is believed that people in the Middle East yearn for peace, compromise, and conciliation. When they don't get it they use violence. But this belief has nothing to do with reality. The problem is that in the Arab/Muslim Middle East peace, compromise, and conciliation are equated with heresy, treason, and surrender.

31. The Arab proverb: "I against my brother, I and my brothers against my cousins, I and my brothers and my cousins against the world" is taken literally and practiced as such.

Examples of this maxim were Saudi and Jordanian assistance to the Yemeni Royalist forces battling an Egyptian intervention force in Yemen (1962-1970), Saudi-Kuwaiti cooperation and assistance in Operation *Desert Storm*–the U.S.-led coalition effort to liberate Kuwait from Iraqi occupation and the 2007 Saudi attempt to build an Arab coalition against Iran's acquisition of nuclear weapons, while at the same time supporting Syria, Iran's ally, in its continued subversion and domination of Lebanon.

32. Arab/Muslim states can always set aside their rivalries and differences for common action against Israel.

The classic example of this maxim in practice occurred in relations between Jordan and Egypt. Between 1957 and 1967 through coup plots, riots, and assassination attempts, Egyptian President Gamal Abdel Nasser tried to topple the Hashemite dynasty of Jordan's King Hussein. The media outlets of both nations were waging a vitriolic propaganda war against each other. **Radio Cairo** referred to the Jordanian monarch as the "Hashemite dwarf" and the "Hashemite whore"–references to King Hussein's small stature and pro-western policy of accepting aid from both the United Kingdom and the United States. In retaliation, **Radio Amman,** mocked Egypt's Nasser for "hiding behind the skirts" of the United Nations Emergency Force in the Sinai Peninsula–a major affront to Arab male pride, accusing one of hiding behind a woman. Yet despite all of this and more, on May 30, 1967, as Nasser gathered Arab armies for the final anticipated destruction of Israel, the Jordanian king flew to Cairo for reconciliation on the tarmac at the Cairo airport, kissing Nasser on the cheeks, and signing a treaty of common defense which placed Jordanian forces under Egyptian command.

33. The Arabs have practiced limited liability war against the Jews in the Land of Israel for over 80 years. They reject any offered compromise, gambling on winning everything by resorting to war, in the comfortable knowledge that even in defeat they will lose nothing. If they lose the war, they then insist on reinstating the original compromise and claim rights under it. When negotiations resume they are based on the original compromise and the Arabs claim additional concessions be made to them.

This has occurred in 1937, 1947, 1949, 1957, 1967, 1973, 1982, 1987, 1993, 2000, and 2006.

34. Throughout the ongoing Arab/Muslim war against Israel, Israel has been forced by pressures, foreign and domestic, to return territory acquired in defensive wars.

This included northern Sinai and southern Lebanon in 1949; all of Sinai and the Gaza Strip in 1957; the Golan-Syrian salient and the Egyptian western shore of the Suez Canal in 1973; all of Sinai, without Egyptian recognition of Jerusalem as Israel's capital between 1974 and 1982; over one-half of Lebanon in 1982; South Lebanon in May 2000, and finally the Gaza Strip in August 2005.

Israel is the sole exception where the international legal principle of *ex injuria jus non oritur* ("right can not originate from wrong") has not been applied. At the end of World War I, aggressor states– Germany, Austria-Hungary, Bulgaria and Turkey–all lost territory, permanently. Similarly after World War II, Germany, Italy, Japan, Romania, Hungary and Finland lost territory, permanently. Only in Israel's case has territory won in a defensive war been removed from the control of a victorious nation.

35. Arab/Muslim forces have historically relied on terrorist unconventional warfare primarily against civilians, especially when confronting a militarily superior foe.

- Active from the 8th to the 14th centuries, the Hashshashin (better known in the West as the Assassins), launched terrorist attacks not only against the Crusaders but also against Muslim rulers. They were followed by the Ainsarii, a sect of

- the Ismaili Assassins who survived the 1256 destruction of the stronghold of Alamut, their mountain fortress located in the central Elburz Mountains, south of the Caspian Sea, in present-day Iran.
- In 1928 the Muslim Brotherhood was formed in Egypt. It attempted to assassinate Egyptian President Gamal Abdel Nasser in 1954. Its influence has spread across the Middle East and into Africa.
- 1949 to date: Muslim terrorists attacked India from Pakistani-controlled Kashmir.
- 1949 to 1956: Arab terror groups operated against Israel from the Egyptian occupied Gaza Strip, and Jordanian occupied Judea and Samaria (what the Arabs call the "West Bank") (See Appendix 18–Judea and Samaria). Collectively they called themselves *fedayeen* from the Arabic *fidā'ī,* which means men of self-sacrifice.
- 1957 to 1967: Arab terror groups operated mainly from Jordanian controlled Judea and Samaria (what the Arabs call the "West Bank"), and occasionally from Syria and Lebanon (See Appendix 19–Israel's insecure borders, 1949-1967 and soon again?).
- During the mid-1960s, and especially after the 1967 Six Day War, Arab terror groups gained notoriety on a worldwide basis thanks to media coverage. Among the many groups were the Palestine Liberation Organization (PLO), an umbrella organization of Palestinian terror groups, which was founded in June 1964. It included many separate groups: Fatah, established in 1959 (and its various subdivisions: Tanzim, the Fatah militia, established in 1995; Force 17, Fatah's elite forces, established in the early 1970s); Hawari,

active from the 1980s to 1991; Ahmed Abu Reish Brigade, an extremist off-shoot of Fatah; the Popular Resistance Committee; Al Aqsa Martyrs Brigades; the Popular Front for the Liberation of Palestine (PFLP), established in 1967; Democratic Front for the Liberation of Palestine (DFLP), established in 1969; and Abu Nidal organization, also known as Fatah-the Revolutionary Council, established in 1974.

There are also Palestinian Arab terrorist groups that are not affiliated with the PLO, including the Popular Front for the Liberation of Palestine-General Command (PFLP-GC), established in 1968; Saiqa, a Syrian-backed Palestinian group; and the Palestine Liberation Front (PLF).

Often a group would appear and after some infamous deed its name would change to protect the perpetrators. An example would be the "Black September" group which committed the infamous massacre of Israeli athletes at the 1972 Munich Olympics. Many of these groups continue their operations to date.

- 1967 to 1970: Terrorist attacks on Israel were launched from Jordan.
- 1970-1982: PLO terrorist attacks were launched against Israel from Lebanon.
- 1970s to date: Al Qaeda terror network conducted activities world-wide.
- 1971-1983: A Marxist-leaning terrorist group known as the Fedayeen (*fadayian* in Persian) was founded in 1971 and based in Tehran. The Fedayeen carried out a number of political assassinations in the course of the struggle that culminated in the Iranian Revolution of 1979.

- Egyptian Islamic Jihad, an offshoot of the Muslim Brotherhood, came to prominence with its assassination of Egyptian President Anwar el-Sadat in October 1981.
- 1983 to date: Hezbollah attacks on Israel from Lebanon and Jewish targets globally
- In 1987, Hamas was founded as an outgrowth of the Muslim Brotherhood. It has been active against Israel since that time.
- 1994 to date: Attacks on Israel from the Palestinian Authority controlled Gaza Strip and PA controlled areas of Judea and Samaria (what the Arabs call the "West Bank")
- Since 2003: Shiite, Sunni, al-Qaeda and foreign terrorist attacks on U.S., coalition forces and Iraqis within Iraq.

36. Since 1973, every Arab state or terrorist organization that has gone to war against Israel has benefited from their aggression.

After the Arab-initiated Yom Kippur War of 1973, Israel gradually withdrew totally from the Sinai Peninsula, and from the Golan Heights eastern salient. After the 1982 PLO war against Israel in Lebanon, Israel withdrew from most of Lebanon and then by May 2000, from southern Lebanon. After the Oslo Accords of 1993, because of Palestinian pledges to stop terrorism and attacks on Israel and its citizens, Israel withdrew from Jericho, Gaza, and later major Arab cities in Judea and Samaria (what the Arabs call the "West Bank"), culminating in a total Israeli withdrawal from the entire Gaza Strip in August 2005.

37. The principle in international law of ex injuria jus non oritur–"right cannot originate from wrong"–i.e.

the aggressor must be punished and penalized applies globally except for Israel.

For aggressive attacks on neighbors, history provides several examples of this principle. At the conclusion of World War I, Germany had to return Schleswig-Holstein to Denmark for its attack on that nation in 1864. Austria-Hungary was stripped of the Southern Tyrol which was given to Italy. Austria-Hungary also lost Slavonia to Yugoslavia at the same time. At the conclusion of World War II, Germany permanently lost Silesia, Pomerania, and southern East Prussia to Poland, and northern East Prussia to the then Soviet Union. Germany further lost the Sudetenland to Czechoslovakia. Japan was stripped of Korea, which became two independent states. Additionally Japan was also stripped of Manchuria, Taiwan, and the Pescadores Islands, all of which were given to China. Italy lost the Dodecanese Islands to Greece for its attack on that nation in 1941.

38. Throughout the conflict between Arab/Muslim forces and the Jewish people in Israel, the Arab/Muslim side has voiced its opposition to Zionism, has tried to equate Zionism with racism, and brand it a colonizing imperialistic ideology.

Zionism is the national desire to re-establish and maintain Jewish sovereignty over the ancient Jewish homeland in Judea. It began with the first Jewish exile in 586 BCE, more than 2,500 years ago.

Zionism is intrinsic in Jewish tradition, nationality and religion. The Zionist ideology advocates regaining sovereignty over the land of their ancestors from which they were exiled by brutal military conquests. There were three such major exiles in Jewish history— in 586 BCE and six hundred fifty-eight years later, in 72 CE, and again in 135 CE. This last historic event, 132-135, was an attempt by the Jewish sage Rabbi Akiva Ben Joseph and his general Shimon Ben-Kotzvah—better known as Shimon Bar Kokhba—to re-establish Jewish sovereignty and rebuild the Temple. The first two exiles were associated with the total destruction of Jerusalem, the ancient Jewish capital, and the demolition of its Temple. In the Bar Kokhba revolt Jerusalem was recaptured but the rebellion was crushed before the Temple could be reconstructed.

The eastern hill of Jerusalem near where the citadel captured by King David once stood, east of the Temple Mount, is called Mount Zion. This name became synonymous with Jerusalem (See Appendix 20–The Jewish connection to Jerusalem); hence Zionism. It should be mentioned that the Jews were expelled from Jerusalem six times in history: by the Chaldeans (New Babylonians) in 586 BCE; the Romans in 72 CE; the Romans again in 135; the Muslim Arabs in 638; the Crusaders in 1099; and from the Old City by the Jordanian Arabs in 1948. Each time their Zionism impelled them to return.

Zionism was not invented at the end of the 19th century. Psalm137 states: "Besides the streams of Babylon we sat and wept at the memory of Zion." Psalm 137 further states: "If I forget thee, O Jerusalem, let my right hand forget her cunning. If I do not remember thee, let my tongue cleave to the roof of my mouth; if I prefer not Jerusalem above my highest joy." These are both twenty-five hundred year-old expressions of Zionism. The Jewish leader Nehemiah was one of the earliest Zionists. His autobiography is the Book of Nehemiah. He built up the walls of Jerusalem to make it militarily defensible and politically autonomous within the Persian Empire.

Akin to the reconstruction of the Temple in Jerusalem and the refortification of the city in the fifth century BCE, when the sovereign Jewish state was reestablished in 1948, Zionism mandated its preservation in perpetuity in its ancient homeland. Any anti-Zionist rhetoric and propaganda is misojudaism (hatred of Jews).

39. Throughout the entire history of the Arab./Muslim war against Israel, the United Nations has been biased, and often hostile to the Jewish state, far from the popular image of being an "impartial" mediator.

The following are but a few of the key examples of UN hostility towards Israel.

- During the 1948-1949 multi-national Arab attack on the newly re-established State of Israel, there were no UN condemnations, no sanctions, or no actions taken to halt the Arab aggression against the Jewish state.
- 1949-1967: The United Nations ignored both Egypt's military occupation of the Gaza Strip and Jordan's illegal occupation of Judea, Samaria and Jerusalem including the Old City; its destruction and desecration of holy sites, and its restrictions on and denial of access to worshippers of all faiths.
- During that same period there were no sanctions or action taken against the many armed attacks against Israel emanating from Jordanian-occupied Judea and Samaria (what the Arabs call the "West Bank"), Egyptian-occupied Gaza and the Syrian-controlled Golan Heights.
- The United Nations Truce Supervisory Organization (UNTSO), which monitored the Arab-Israeli armistice lines from 1949 to 1970, did little more than report outbreaks of violence. In fact, on June 5, 1967, UNTSO allowed Jordanian

forces to occupy UNTSO positions at Government House in Jerusalem, which the Jordanians used to open fire against the Israeli-controlled parts of the city. Later, during the 1000 Day War of Attrition, 1967-1970, UNTSO sat at the Suez Canal–failing to stop the Egyptian attacks on Israeli-controlled Sinai.

- In 1951 there were no UN sanctions or actions taken to enforce the Security Council resolution which condemned .25Egypt's illegal closure of the Suez Canal (See Appendix 21–The Constantinople Convention on Free Navigation of the Suez Canal) to Israeli ships and cargoes.
- From 1951-1954, while Egypt tightened its blockade of the Strait of Tiran against Israeli ships and cargoes, there was no UN action taken over this denial of the right of free passage in international waters.
- The United Nations Emergency Force (UNEF) was established at the close of the Sinai-Suez War of 1956. Its mission was to maintain the peace along the Egyptian-Israel Armistice line and keep the Strait of Tiran open to all nations, including Israel. Shockingly, the most infamous act perpetrated by UNEF occurred in mid-May 1967. At that time Egyptian President Gamal Abdel Nasser mobilized his army and sent it to the Egyptian-Israeli frontier. Nasser ordered the United Nations Emergency Force (UNEF) to leave immediately and incredulously, UN Secretary General U Thant complied within three days. This despite long standing international agreements that there would be deliberations if and when the UNEF had completed its mission and was to be removed.

In the symbolic style of Neville Chamberlain, when the storm clouds of war appeared, the UNEF folded its umbrella and quietly stole away. This UNEF withdrawal paved the way for Nasser's blockade of the Strait of Tiran, an act of war, which in turn triggered the Six Day War in early June 1967.

- In 1964, Syria, Jordan, and Lebanon began to divert the headwaters of the Jordan River, to deny Israel its main water source. Again, there was no condemnation, no sanctions, and no action taken by the United Nations.
- From the early 1970s repeated Palestine Liberation Organization (PLO) terrorist attacks were launched from southern Lebanon against Israel. The PLO had established a virtual state-within-a-state–" Fatahland " (a precursor to the current "Hezbollahland" of today)–to attack Israeli towns and civilians. The United Nations as usual did nothing.
- When Israel launched a limited reprisal raid into southern Lebanon in March 1978, the UN responded with the creation of the United Nations Interim Force in Lebanon (UNIFIL), which for the next 28 years would not keep the peace. Instead, UNIFIL would sit passively as terrorist attacks continued from Lebanon into Israel, first by the PLO and then after 1983, by Hezbollah. Through the years UNIFIL provided human shields from behind which Hezbollah could plan and launch further attacks. In an episode that showed UNIFIL's actual cooperation with Hezbollah, they filmed a Hezbollah abduction of three Israeli soldiers and refused to release the footage to the public.
- After the 2006 Second Lebanon War, the UNIFIL was made into a more "robust" force with the declared purpose of disarming Hezbollah, preventing the return of Hezbollah terrorist forces to the Lebanese-Israeli border, and to interdict the flow of weaponry to Hezbollah and other groups from

Syria. UNIFIL has failed miserably on all counts as Hezbollah has re-armed to higher levels than before the 2006 Second Lebanon War. Today Hezbollah is back in greater numbers both in men and weaponry than before the war. The flow of sophisticated armaments moves unimpeded from Iran and Syria into Lebanon.

While the United Nations peacekeepers in the Middle East have supplied the world with a veritable alphabet soup of acronyms, they have conducted no real peacekeeping. The United Nations record is dismal, with the term "peacekeeping" becoming an oxymoron.

This is but the tip of the iceberg of United Nations ineptness, bias, and hostility towards Israel. Not to be overlooked is the fact that after 1965 the United Nations General Assembly came to be dominated by the Arab-African-Asian-Communist bloc, which was joined in increasing numbers by European nations. This amalgam exercised what U.S. Ambassador to the United Nations, Daniel Patrick Moynihan so aptly termed "The tyranny of the majority." Literally hundreds. of anti-Israel resolutions have come from the General Assembly. These included:

- In December 1970, after seven PLO terrorist attacks during the previous seven months, the General Assembly passed a resolution recognizing the "inalienable rights of the Palestinian people."
- On November 13, 1974, PLO chief Yasir Arafat was allowed to speak at the UN General Assembly, becoming the first non-state leader to do so.

- On November 22, 1974, nine days later, the UN granted permanent representative "observer" status in effect, ***de facto*** member privileges (albeit without voting rights) to the PLO, the world's leading terrorist organization. Passing, in 1975, the infamous UN General Assembly Resolution 3379 equating Zionism with racism. It would not be until December 16, 1991, that the UN General Assembly passed Resolution 4686 which rescinded UNGA 3379 by a vote of 111-25, with 13 abstentions and 17 absent or not voting. It should be stressed that this has been the only anti-Israel resolution revoked to date (See Appendix 23–UN Zionism is Racism Resolution and its repeal).

NEGOTIATIONS

40. The Jews/Israelis have consistently attempted to reach a fair compromise with their Arab/Muslim enemies only to be rejected time and time again.

Since 1913 there have been several compromise offers made, of Arab statehood that would enable them to live side by side with the Jewish state. These offers were made by the Jewish community, in Israel and abroad, the British, the United Nations, the Americans, or some combination thereof. To list the most notable examples:

- 1913: Hochberg-Yahrawi understanding at the First Arab Congress.
- 1918: Weizmann-Suleiman Bey Nassir understanding in Cairo.
- 1919: Feisal-Weizmann agreement at the Paris Peace Conference.
- 1937: Peel Commission offer of partition (offered 20% of Western Palestine to the Jews; the Arabs rejected the plan).
- 1938: Woodhead Commission (offered less to the Jews; but the Arabs rejected the offer and attacked the Jewish community even before it declared independence in 1948).
- 1947: UN Partition Plan (See Appendix 24–UN Partition plan).

- 1949: Rhodes Armistice talks, and Lausanne, Paris, and Geneva Conferences.
- 1954-1955: U.S.-sponsored Johnston Plan to share the waters of the Jordan Valley basin. Accepted by Israel, rejected by the Arabs.
- 1967: Post Six Day War Israel Peace Initiative at the United Nations, rejected by the "Three No's" of the Arab Summit Conference at Khartoum, Sudan.
- 1970: The Allon Plan, semi-officially held by Israel's Labor governments up until their electoral defeat in 1977; envisaged Israeli annexation of the Jordan Valley and areas around Jerusalem as well as the return of most of Judea-Samaria to the Jordanians.
- 1979: Camp David treaty with Egypt; an offer to Palestinian Arab leadership; Israeli settlements dismantled in Sinai; Sinai returned to Egypt.
- 1983: Israel-Lebanon treaty invalidated following assassination of President Bashir Gemayel.
- 1993: Oslo Accords.
- 1994: Israel-Jordan Peace Treaty, territory ceded to Jordan.
- 1995: Oslo II.
- June 2000: Israeli Prime Minister Ehud Barak's offer, at Camp David II, to cede 97% of the territories. Rejected by Yasir Arafat who launched the Al Aqsa Intifada.
- December 2000: President Bill Clinton's offer (Oval Office Bridge Plan) during the Al Aqsa Intifada.
- January 2001: Israeli offer at Taba Talks and at the Davos Conference during Al Aqsa Intifada. Arafat's rejection.
- June 24, 2002: President George W. Bush: "If you want your state, stop the terror." The Palestinian terrorism continued.

- April 2004: The Quartet's Road Map—stop terror and incitement, but both continued.
- April 14, 2004: Israeli Prime Minister Sharon's unilateral offer of Statehood.
- August 2005: Unilateral Israeli withdrawal from the Gaza Strip, including uprooting 21 Israeli communities and forcible relocation of 9,000 Israelis.

In contrast, in November 1977, Egyptian President Anwar el-Sadat famously addressed the Israeli Knesset. His words had different meanings than the way they were understood by his Israeli audience and the Western world.

The West must understand that words, including "peace," "freedom," "tyranny," and "justice" are understood differently by Islam and the Western democracies.

For the Muslim world, "freedom" means freedom from foreign domination or influence. Israel is viewed as "foreign." It was the foreign domination, including so-called Israeli "occupation" that produced "tyranny." "Justice" is the elimination of this "tyranny" which means the elimination of Israel.

Sadat, in his speech, kept repeating that peace must be based on "justice." He used the word fifteen times in that one speech and defined justice as Israel's disappearance. "Justice," said Sadat, required Israel to give up all the territories taken in the 1967 conflict and the return of Palestinian Arab refugees. The fulfillment of those conditions would guarantee that Israel would cease to exist as a Jewish state. Sadat also proclaimed that Jewish independence in Palestine was illegitimate in its totality stating "the land did not belong to you."

The "peace and justice" which Sadat offered Israel in his speech, was really only *dhimmi* rights in a Muslim Palestine. It would be an Israeli surrender to the conditions imposed by Islam. It is in this context to which the Arab/Muslim world ascribes. There can be no diplomatic solution as long as the goal of one side–the Arabs–remains the annihilation of the other–Israel.

41. The Arab/Muslim countries practice bazaar diplomacy.

The rule in the bazaar is that if the vendor knows that you desire to purchase a piece of merchandize, he will raise its price. The Arabs sell words; e.g. "peace" and "security." They sign agreements including "peace treaties," and they trade with vague promises; e.g. stopping terrorist acts. They demand tangible concessions; e.g., territorial withdrawals, prisoner releases, restrictions on access to Holy places, demands for money, and arms, from eager Israeli governments seeking the intangibles mentioned above. The side that first presents his terms and concessions is bound to lose; the other side builds his next demand(s) using the opening offers of his opponent as the starting point. In the Arab-Israeli conflict, the two sides are not discussing the same merchandise. The Israelis wish to acquire peace based on the Arab/Muslim acceptance of Israel as a Jewish state. The objective of the Arab/Muslim side is to annihilate the Jewish state, replace it with an Arab state, and get rid of the Jews.

In Middle Eastern bazaar diplomacy, agreements are kept not because they are signed but because they are imposed. "Reciprocity" in negotiations between Israel and the Arabs is impossible. It is simply foreign to the Arab mind. This indicates that Arabs, unlike Jews and people in the West, lack the cultural ability to see or respect the other fellow's point of view and to moderate their demands accordingly.

An intrinsic part of negotiating is the practice of ***sumuh***-"steadfastness." It is the practice to wait as long as it takes to wear down one's opponent, until he is ready to abandon the struggle. Under this practice the Arabs/Muslims are prepared to wait decades, generations, even centuries to achieve their goals. A classic historic example is the Muslim attempts to rid the Middle East of the Crusader states, which took 193 years. The concept of ***sumuh***-"steadfastness"- can be seen in the on-going process, starting with Sadat's visit to Jerusalem in 1977, Arafat's demands, and the Saudi demands via their "peace plan" of 2002-all have the same goal.

Western foreign policy and culture in general always is in a hurry, seeking a quick solution to problems. The West has been willing to settle for less in order to make a deal now. The Arabs/Muslims on the other hand want exactly what they want and are willing to wait for it. The Arab/Muslim side has not made a secret of the fact that what they meant by the word "peace" was nothing more than a limited ceasefire-a ***hudna*** (truce or cease-fire) for a limited period. Therefore it is most important for a nation to be prepared for war. It should never come to the negotiating table from a position of weakness. Your adversary should always know that you are strong and ready for war even more than you are ready for peace.

42. What is privately promised in a non-Middle Eastern language, during negotiations, is inconsequential. What is stated publicly in Arabic or Farsi is what counts.

The best illustration of this, was Yasir Arafat, who after negotiating with the Israelis returned to his people and proclaimed "Jihad, Jihad, Jihad, Jihad" as the only way to gain control of all of Israel. The video clip is seen in the recent films: *Obsession: Radical Islam's War against the West* and *Farewell Israel*.

43. There is an Arab proverb which states: "There is no tax on words." It succinctly expresses the negotiating style of the Arab/Muslim Middle East.

Woven into this style is the Arab concept of **taqiyya** (deception) and the Arab tactic of **darura** (necessity). Necessity can justify even violating explicit prohibitions in Islam, as long as they are done to protect the faith. Thus one may lie–lie even about Islam itself, negotiate with infidels, deal with foreign women as "equals" (e.g. Secretaries of State Condolezza Rice, Madelaine Albright, and Speaker of the House Nancy Pelosi), eat pork–all to gain the goal sought. It is "the end justifies the means," Middle East style.

The Treaty of Al-Hudaybiyya concluded by Muhammad's state of Medina and the Quraysh tribe of Mecca in March 628 CE was the role model for all subsequent Arab/Muslim negotiations. In this treaty Muhammad promised a 10-year cease-fire with the Meccans but Muhammad broke the treaty within two years and attacked and conquered Mecca.

In the modern period, the list of agreements made and then broken by Arabs/Muslims, to further their position, included the following. They are examples of *taqiyya*–"deception" by word.

- The 1949 Arab-Israeli armistice agreement which included cessation of hostilities and access to all holy places–both violated.
- During the Sinai-Suez War, the "cease-fire" called by the Governor of Port Said, Egypt in face of advancing Anglo-French forces–was promptly repudiated hours later.
- The 1957 memorandum of understanding between Egyptian President Gamal Abdel Nasser and UN Secretary General Dag Hammarskjold concluded at the end of the Sinai-Suez War—which guaranteed free passage for Israeli shipping through the Strait of Tiran and provided guidelines as to how the United Nations Emergency Force (UNEF), was to be removed in the future–was subsequently "lost" and broken by Egypt.
- The 1970 cease-fire agreement between Egypt and Israel, ending the 1967-1970 1000 Day War of Attrition, and guaranteed by the United States and the Soviet Union, was violated overnight by both Egypt and the Soviet Union.
- The 1974 Israel-Egypt Disengagement Agreement, which limited artillery batteries to be had by both sides and allowed Israeli cargoes through the Suez Canal, was broken and violated by Egypt.
- The 1975 Algiers Agreement between Iraq and Iran (under the Shah), ending their boundary dispute over the Shatt Al-Arab and support for the Kurds–was broken by Iraq five years later.

- The 1991 United Nations Mission for a Referendum in Western Sahara (MINURSO) was originally agreed to by the parties, including Morocco. No referendum on the future of Western Sahara, first scheduled for 1992, was held to date, because of Moroccan objections.
- The Oslo Accords of August 20, 1993, signed between Israel and the Palestine Liberation Organization calling for an end to terrorist attacks against Israel as well as removal of the clauses in the PLO Charter explicitly calling for Israel's destruction–was never honored by the PLO.
- The Hebron Protocol of January 1997, between Israel and the Palestinian Authority, which called for a cessation of terrorism against Israel–was not implemented.
- The Wye River Memorandum of October 1998–which yet again called for the implementation of the two previous agreements including an end to terrorist attacks on Israel– was again ignored.

One must recall the words of President John F. Kennedy, who emphasized that **"Peace does not exist in signed documents and treaties alone, but in the hearts and minds of the people."** Whereas the Israelis have long been desirous of peace, the Arab/Muslim side has sought the elimination of Israel, directly or indirectly, immediately or in stages, by military means or by "negotiations."

44. There is also taqiyya–"deception" applied to Arab/Muslim deeds. The Hadidth Volume 4, Book 52, Number 269 states: (Narrated by Jabir bin 'Abdellah) The Prophet (Mohammad) said, "War is deceit."

A few modern examples of this include:

- During the First Lebanese Civil War of 1958, United Nations Secretary General Dag Hammarskjold visited that nation in mid-June to ascertain, firsthand, if the United Arab Republic was intervening in the civil war and aiding the rebels seeking to overthrow the legitimate government of President Camille Chamoun. As part of his inspection, Hammarskjold was taken to the Basta–the Muslim section of Beirut, the capital. The Basta was already in the hands of the rebels and the UAR flag flew over that section of the city. For Hammarskjold's visit, however, all UAR flags were removed and replaced with Lebanese banners. As soon as he left, up went the UAR flags. "Volunteers" from the UAR, arms, war materials and financing continued unopposed.
- On July 16, 1972, Egyptian President Anwar el-Sadat publicly "expelled" the over 21,000 Soviet military advisers based in Egypt. (The International Institute for Strategic Studies stated that only 3,000 had left). This was part of Sadat's grand deception in preparation for war with Israel, planned for the next year. The Israelis felt that the expulsion of the Soviet military advisers significantly reduced the effectiveness of the Egyptian army. In reality, while some Soviet personnel had left Egypt because their training mission was complete, others left while new advisors took their place. It was more a military rotation of duty than an "expulsion."

- In mid-May 1973, Egypt staged huge war games on the west side of the Suez Canal. Troops were positioned, and ramps were constructed down to the water's edge–all part of the preparations for offensive war against Israel on the opposite bank of the canal. The Israelis counter-mobilized. The effort cost Israel $14 million. Egypt then stopped its preparations and seemingly reduced the number of its forces and preparations—but not in reality. Had the Israelis not counter-mobilized, what came to be known as the Yom Kippur War would probably have erupted in the late spring rather than the early autumn. In any event Egypt applied the same tactics in early October. This time the Israelis assumed it was just another series of war games and not wanting to disrupt its economy, spend the money and counter-mobilize its citizen army, Israel did nothing until it was too late and the Yom Kippur War erupted October 6, 1973, catching Israel by surprise. Egypt's Sadat was hailed throughout the Arab world as "The Master of taqiyya–Deception."
- On October 6, 1981, Egyptian President Anwar el-Sadat was reviewing a military parade celebrating the Egyptian successes in the Yom Kippur War. Part of the military procession, was in fact an Egyptian Islamic Jihad assassination team, which had infiltrated the Egyptian army. It caught Egyptian security by surprise and was able to kill the Egyptian leader.

45. *In the Islamic Middle East, the rational desire for peace is often perceived as weakness, a despised trait in that culture.*

From the outset it must be understood that the term "peace" is viewed differently by the Islamic world and the West. The word ***salaam*** is thought, by many in the West, including Israelis, to mean "peace." It does not. It means an absence of conflict or in modern parlance a truce–a ***hudna*** in Arabic. The Arabic word ***sulha***—which means "reconciliation" is closer to the Western concept of peace, but is used only between two Muslim parties. In the case of recognition of Israel as a Jewish state in the Middle East, there can never be ***sulha***.

The Israeli government from the late 1980s was obsessed with "peace." Labor Party leaders, Shimon Peres and Yitzhak Rabin envisioned a "new Middle East" with countries living beside one another in peace, as in modern Europe. They forgot they were not living in Switzerland with Liechtenstein and Austria as neighbors, but rather in one of the roughest, toughest, and most dangerous "neighborhoods" in the world. Their neighbors are Hamas in Gaza, Fatah in Judea-Samaria, Syria, and Hezbollah-Iranian-Syrian dominated Lebanon, to name a few. These Israeli leaders deluded themselves into thinking that peace could be achieved by returning disputed lands acquired in a war of self-defense. Both men believed **"You can only make peace with enemies."** That **"If it doesn't work the whole world will support us."** They were naïve and displayed Israeli weakness again and again. As recent events have proved, Israel got neither peace nor the understanding and support of the world. The Israeli leadership seems intent on living out George Orwell's observation that **"the quickest way of ending a war is to lose it."**

Thus Israel, under its Labor government, negotiated the Oslo Accords, which rescued a defeated and discredited PLO; brought it back from exile in Tunisia, allowing the PLO a territorial base; supplied it with weapons and ammunition; freed terrorists to rejoin their PLO comrades; provided an infrastructure–port facilities, airport, water, electricity, radio and television stations–even a postal system; and encouraged the United States and the European Union to lavish billions of dollars in aid to the newly created "Palestinian Authority." All this was given to the Arabs, for Yasir Arafat's verbal promise of "peace" and "two states for two peoples." But while the Israelis were deluding themselves Arafat was telling the entire Arab world that this was all part of the strategy of stages. He continued to urge *jihad, jihad, jihad, jihad;* claim that Jerusalem–all of it–belonged to the Palestinian Arabs; and make it explicitly clear that "peace for land" did not mean security (for Israel) for land.

Terrorism, a second intifada– the Al Aqsa Intifada–and non-stop rocketing of Israel was the result. When the Al Aqsa Intifada began, the IDF general staff began to prepare a response called Operation *Thorns,* a plan for the retaking of the PA areas. They estimated Israeli dead at 300. But the Israeli government chose to do nothing. Since then there have been more than 1,500 Jews killed, which is five times the estimated combat deaths (plus 10,000 wounded, many maimed for life), with no apparent consequences to the terrorists' ability to inflict casualties on Israel. As Israelis died in suicide bombings, Israeli Prime Minister Yitzhak Rabin incredulously remarked that such Israeli deaths were **"the price for peace."** Israeli governments had become accomplices in the Arab diplomatic offensive designed to reduce Israel territorially and demographically in stages, weakening Israel's resolve and de-Zionize it.

As recently as April 2008, the PLO/Palestinian strategy of "stages" or "phases" was re-emphasized by the PA representative in Lebanon, Abbas Zaki. Zaki, also known as Sharif Mash'al, was a former head of Fatah operations, stated in an interview with NBN TV, as reported by MEMRI, April 14, 2008: "The PLO is the sole legitimate representative [of the Palestinian people], and it has not changed its platform even one iota. . . . the PLO proceeds through phases, without changing its strategy. Let me tell you, when the ideology of Israel collapses, and we take, at last, Jerusalem, the Israeli ideology will collapse in its entirety, and we will begin to progress with our own ideology, Allah willing, and drive them out of all of Palestine."

All this is leading to the transition of Israelis from living in a sovereign Jewish state, to being degraded to **dhimmi** status within a Muslim state. Only part of the Israelis will accept this change, others will be killed or go into exile again.

Further examples of this principle (Al Aqsa Intifada, Lebanon, Iraq-Iran, and Gaza) are found above in Rules #27, 35, and 39.

SECURITY

46. Security barriers are not obstacles to peace.

Security barriers have been constructed throughout history, from the Great Wall of China to the security barrier between Israel and Gaza built in 1994. Some other notable security barriers are listed below in chronological order:

- North Korea/South Korea: The 151-mile-long demilitarized zone has separated the two Koreas since 1953 and is the most heavily fortified border in the world.
- Belfast, Derry, and other areas of Northern Ireland: The "Peace Line," is a series of barriers first constructed in the early 1970s to curb escalating violence between Catholic and Protestant neighborhoods. The barriers range from a few hundred feet to over three miles in length. By 2006, there were more than 40 such barriers spanning a total distance of over 13 miles in Belfast, Derry, and other areas.
- Oman: On June 9, 1965, a rebellion began in Oman's Dhofar Province, led by the Dhofar Liberation Front (DLF) against the central government. The guerrillas were supported by the People's Democratic Republic of (South) Yemen (PDRY) and backing the PDRY was the Soviet Union. In response, in late

1973, the Omani government constructed the Hornbeam Line, a 31 mile barbed wire fence. As the conflict continued Oman had to construct another barrier to the southwest of the Hornbeam Line,—the Damavand Line, which consisted of a double barbed wire with mines.

- Cyprus: Since 1974, Turkey has constructed and maintains a 187-mile separation barrier–the Attila Line–along the 1974 cease-fire line dividing Cyprus into two parts. The barrier is made of concrete, barbed wire, watchtowers, minefields, and ditches. This was done in violation of several United Nations Security Council resolutions.

- Morocco/Western Sahara: This barrier called the "Berm" or "Moroccan Wall" is a series of ten-foot-high sand and stone barriers, some mined, and run for 1,678 miles through the Western Sahara. Today there are six separate sets of walls constructed between August 1980 and April 1987. They are intended to keep Polisario guerrillas out of the Morocco-occupied and controlled Western Sahara.

- India/Bangladesh: India began in 1986, to construct a 2,043-mile barbed wire barrier surrounding its neighbor to prevent smuggling, illegal immigration, and infiltration by terrorists. The estimated cost by the time of its completion is $1.2 billion.

- India/Pakistan: In 1989 India began erecting a 330-mile separation barrier along the 460-mile disputed 1972 "Line of Control" between Indian and Pakistani-controlled Kashmir. Its purpose is to stop arms smuggling, infiltration by Pakistani-based Islamist separatists, and terrorists into Indian-controlled Kashmir. The fence is electrified barbed and concertina wire eight to twelve feet high. That barrier was completed in late 2004. According to Indian military sources, the fence has reduced by 80% the numbers of terrorists who routinely cross into India to attack soldiers and civilians.

- Kuwait/Iraq: The 120-mile demilitarized zone along this border has been manned by UN soldiers and observers since the Gulf War I ended, in 1991. Made of electric fencing and wire, and supplemented by fifteen-foot-wide trenches, the barrier extends from Saudi Arabia to the Persian Gulf. In 2006 Kuwait decided to install an additional 135-mile iron partition.
- Uzbekistan/Afghanistan: The Uzbek-Afghan barrier is a separation barrier built in the early 1990s by Uzbekistan along its 130-mile border with Afghanistan. It consists of a barbed wire fence, a second taller electrified barbed-wire fence, as well as land mines.
- United States/Mexico: In the mid-1990s, President Bill Clinton initiated two programs, Operation **Gatekeeper** in California and Operation **Hold the Line,** in Texas, to crack down on illegal immigration from Mexico. They produced a system of high-tech barriers, including a fourteen-mile fence separating San Diego from Tijuana. On October 26, 2006, the U.S. Congress passed the Security Fence Act which calls for the construction of 700 miles of security fence along its border with Mexico.
- Uzbekistan/Kyrgyzstan: In 1999 Uzbekistan began construction of a barbed wire fence to secure their border with Kyrgyzstan and prevent terrorist infiltration.
- Botswana/Zimbabwe: In 2003 the government of Botswana started construction of a 300-mile ten-foot-high electric fence along its border with Zimbabwe to control the spread

of foot-and-mouth disease. Zimbabwe claims that the fence really aims to curb the immigration flow from troubled Zimbabwe into stable and calm Botswana.
- Saudi Arabia/Yemen: In 2003 Saudi Arabia began building a ten foot-high barrier along part of its 1,118-mile border with Yemen to prevent terrorist infiltration. In February 2004, Saudi Arabia halted construction due to Yemeni objections that the fence violated a border treaty signed in 2000.
- United Arab Emirates/Oman: a separation barrier constructed by the UAE along its border with Oman is an effort to curb the flow of illegal migrants, illicit drugs, and terrorists.
- Pakistan/Afghanistan: On December 26, 2006, Pakistan announced it would fence and mine part of its 1,500-mile border to stop Islamofascist terrorists and drug smugglers. The Afghan government objects the Pakistani move since it would legitimize the international recognized Durand Line (drawn in 1893 by the British).
- Brunei/Malaysia: Brunei is currently building a security fence along its 12 ½ -mile border with Limbang, Sarawak, Malaysia to stop smuggling and the flow of illegal immigrants.
- Egypt has built a security fence around Sharm el-Sheikh in Sinai, to prevent future terrorist attacks on the tourist resort town.
- Iran/Pakistan: Iran has begun construction of a separation barrier along its border with Pakistan to stop illegal border crossings, curb the flow of drugs, and to stop terrorist attacks. The wall will be 3 ft thick and 10 ft high made of concrete reinforced with steel rods and will cover the 435-mile (700 km) border between the two nations.
- Saudi Arabia/Iraq: In 2006 Saudi Arabia announced plans for the construction of a security fence along the entire length of

its 560 mile desert border with Iraq to secure the kingdom's borders.
- Thailand/Malaysia: Thailand plans to build a concrete fence along parts of its southern border with Malaysia to keep Islamist terrorists and dual citizens from crossing the Thai frontier.

In response to the increased terrorism, including suicide bombings, after the start of the Al-Aqsa Intifada in September 2000, Israel began construction of a security barrier as a necessary measure of passive self-defense. The barrier, bordering Judea and Samaria (what the Arabs call the "West Bank") is planned for a total distance of 436 miles (703 kilometers). To date only 58% of the barrier has been built. It may not be completed until 2010 due to lack of funding.

While Arab supporters continuously call this barrier, a "wall", and an "obstacle to peace," in reality the vast majority of the barrier, over 385 miles is comprised of wire fences, vehicle barriers, and electronic sensors. The remaining 30-foot-high concrete sections being built are designed to block three areas where Arab snipers have shot at houses in border villages as well as cars traveling on the trans-Israel highway, and around the Biblical matriarch Rachel's Tomb, just south of Jerusalem.

Thus far, the barrier has worked. Since its construction began, there has been a 90-percent decrease in terrorist attacks. The Israeli barrier is not an obstacle to peace. It is just one of many partitions around the world aimed at repelling invaders whether they are terrorists, guerrillas, or illegal immigrants.

MEDIA

47. There is no such thing as a free press in the Arab/Muslim Middle East. According to the Islamic Mass Media Charter, adopted by the First International Islamic Mass Media Conference in Jakarta in 1980, Muslim media professionals are to "censor all material which is either broadcast or published, in order to protect the *umma* (the Islamic world-wide community) from influences which are harmful to Islamic character and values, and in order to forestall all dangers," *and to preserve the integrity of the profession and Islamic traditions.* **Muslim media professionals are "committed to the propagation of** *da'wah* **(propagation of the faith), to elucidating Islamic issues and to the defense of the Muslim point of view."**

Any Western news media coverage is subject to strict regulation and guidelines. Reporters, photographers and video crews cannot travel freely. They are guided by "handlers" who tell them where they can visit, who they can interview (usually individuals who will echo the "party line"), and what pictures or videos they can take. More often than not, scenes are staged for the cameras. Any reporter straying from the guidelines will never be allowed into that country or area again or worse still, suffer consequences including imprisonment or even death.

To illustrate, during the first *intifada* that erupted in December 1987, foreign correspondents, including those from NBC and CNN freely admitted that many events were staged and falsified for the media cameras. Similar activities took place during the second Al Aqsa Intifada that began in September 2000. One of the most outrageous episodes was the alleged shooting death of Muhammad al-Dura hiding behind his father by Israeli forces, which was televised globally. Subsequent investigations have shown that the carefully edited *France 2* video was wholly inconclusive, that al-Dura could not have been hit by Israeli fire and has since been proven to be false. In other words—it was a staged event and there is even doubt that al-Dura himself, was killed.

On June 9, 2006, an explosion on a Gaza beach killed seven Palestinian family members. Shortly afterward, Palestinian Authority television released a horrific video showing a ten-year-old girl shrieking amidst the bodies. Palestinian hospital workers and spokesmen angrily blamed Israel Defense Forces artillery fire—even though no investigation had been conducted, and the accusers had no way of knowing what caused the explosion. It was ultimately determined that the family was not killed by the IDF. Rather, Hamas had mined the area to defend their arsenal of Qassam rockets against Israeli commandos.

The video was a twisted amalgam of spliced footage and questionable anachronisms, quite simply, a fake. The explosion occurred some ten minutes after the last Israeli shell had been fired into the area. The shrapnel in the bodies was not from Israeli ordnance. Hamas had almost certainly killed its own but then immediately blamed Israel.

Although the 2006 Second Lebanon War was initiated by the aggressive acts of Hezbollah–first, kidnapping two Israeli soldiers and then unleashing the barrage of over 4,000 missiles against Israel–Hezbollah was able through manipulation of the media, to portray itself and Lebanon as the "victims" of the conflict. When Israeli bombs went astray and killed civilians–as they did in the town of Qana on July 30–Hezbollah media handlers quickly descended on the scene to manage the coverage, positioning props, most famously a child's teddy bear, and parade bandaged casualties, and ashen-gray fatalities. The teddy bear was clean (therefore not at the building when it was struck), and the so called deceased had died of other causes, but were brought to the scene to be displayed as alleged bombing victims. Hezbollah was thus able to turn world opinion against Israel, the real victim of the onslaught.

It should further be noted that many journalists have only superficial knowledge of the Middle East–its long history, and culture. Few reporters speak Arabic, Farsi, Turkish, or Hebrew and therefore they cannot check out to confirm information provided by PR personnel of the local authorities. Moreover, understanding discussions among the "handlers" could readily reveal falsifications. The media, which could send knowledgeable reporters to cover the news, prefer not to do so.

48. Arab-Islamic indoctrination is a highly successful industry, well organized and without opposition. It makes use of misinformation, manipulation, omission of key facts, lack of context, oversimplification of complex issues and historical inaccuracy.

In recent coverage of events in the Middle East, the Arabs limit their discussion of the region to the period after the 1967 Six Day War. Omitted from such coverage is reference to the Jordanian occupation of Judea and Samaria (what the Arabs call the "West Bank") and the Egyptian occupation of the Gaza Strip. Only Arab refugees are referred to, ignoring the far larger number of Jewish refugees from Arab/Muslim nations (See Appendix 26–Jewish Population in Arab countries).

Most recently the Iranian President Mahmoud Ahmadinejad told an audience at Columbia University in New York on September 24, 2007: **"We don't have homosexuals like in your country. We don't have that in our country. We don't have this phenomenon; I don't know who's told you we have it."** At face value that may be true as they are put to death in that nation. According to the Iranian gay and lesbian rights group Homan, the Iranian government has put to death an estimated 4,000 homosexuals since 1980.

49. *The use of specific vocabulary can, over time, change reality to fiction, obliterate history, and create new "truths" from the fabric of the big lie technique, perfected by Nazi Propaganda Chief Joseph Goebbels who declared, "If you tell a lie big enough and keep repeating it, people will eventually come to believe it."*

TABLE 6
The war of words

WHAT THE ARABS AND THEIR SUPPORTERS SAY	WHAT IS HISTORICALLY CORRECT
"Palestinian-Israeli conflict"	Arab-Muslim war against Israel and the Jewish people; and the Israeli frontline in the war of Islamofascism ★ against the West
"Creation of the state of Israel"	Re-establishment of a sovereign Israel
"anti-Zionist" and "anti-Zionism"	Misojudaic and misojudaism (hatred of Jews)
"Greater Israel"	Land of Israel; Eretz Yisrael
"Occupied territories"	Disputed territories
"Palestine"	Land of Israel
Palestinians	Arabs in Judea, Samaria, and Gaza
Al Quds	Jerusalem
Nablus	Shchem
Umm Rashrash	Eilat
"The West Bank"	Judea and Samaria
"settlers"	residents
"settlements"	communities or towns and villages
"illegal outposts"	unauthorized housing
'the Wall"	the security barrier
"militants, guerrillas, freedom fighters"	terrorists, assassins, murderers
shaheed (martyr)	suicide murderer

"The *Nakhba* (The Disaster)"	Outcome of Arab aggression (The Israeli War of Independence)
"The October (Ramadan) War 1973"	The Yom Kippur War 1973
The Second–Al Aqsa Intifada	The Oslo War
"The Wailing Wall"	The Western Wall of the Second Temple
"IOF" (Israeli Occupation Forces)	IDF (Israeli Defense Force)

★ Islamofascism as a term was introduced by French writer Maxine Rodinson (1945-2004) to describe the Iranian Revolution of 1979. The pairing of the two words "Islamic" and "'fascism" conveys a precise message. The old fascism is back, but is now driven by a radical fundamentalist ideology of Islam. Islamofascism is the *jihadist* Islamic ideology grafted onto the totalitarian dictatorial system of fascism, where the goals of Islam are more important than the rights of individuals. It has an anti-humanist character. It seeks to re-create a mystical past (the Caliphate). It is anti-democratic, populist, expansive (imperialistic), aggressive, and glorifies war–*jihad*. Violence, intimidation, belligerent *jihadist* Islam, superiority over non-believers (racism), misojudaism (hatred of Jews), and anti-liberalism are components of this ideology.

Conservatively, an estimated 20% of the world's 1.3 - 1.5 billion Muslims can be classified as Islamofascists. That is 260-300 million Islamofascists, a group equal roughly to the population of the United States. Every political, economic, diplomatic and military "victory" brings more adherents to the Islamofascist cause. On November 30, 2005, former U.S. Secretary of State Henry Kissinger stated simply what angers the Islamofascists: "What provokes the Islamofascists is our existence– not our policies." The war against Islamofascism will be long and can end in the defeat of the Islamofascists–but only if we can summon the will to see and understand what is at stake.

As Dietrich Bonhoeffer, Christian theologian, who was hanged by the Nazis for his views stated: "Failure of people to speak small truths results in victory of the Big Lie."

50. Transliterating Arabic words and phrases into their precise English phonetic equivalents is an exercise of great complexity.

To illustrate:- The Saudi city on the Red Sea known as Jeddah may be transliterated as: Jadda, Jaddah, Jedda, Jeddah, Jidda, Jiddah, Judda, Juddah, Djiddah, Djuddah, Djouddah, Gedda, Dsjiddah, Djettah, or Dscheddah. All are acceptable!

In a study of the Middle East one will find many such different yet acceptable transliterations.

To cite but a few:

Faisal = Feisal = Faysal
Koran = Qur'an = Q'run
Ramadan = Ramadhan = Ramzan
Abu Dhabi = Abu Zaby
Quneitra = Qunaytirah = Kuneitra
Qadhafi = Khaddafi = Gaddafi

Abdellah = Abdallah = Abd'Allah
bedouin = badawin
Mohammed = Muhammad

Dubai = Dubayy
Mecca = Makkah

CONCLUSION

By a careful reading of these "Rules of Thumb" the reader will obtain a deeper understanding of the complexities of the Middle East, its history, politics, diplomacy, and culture. As ever-unfolding events continue to stream out of that troubled section of the world, this book will continue to provide guidelines and serve as a frame of reference.

APPENDIX 1
VITAL WATERWAYS

THE STRAITS

- *The Bosporus:* 16 miles long; 1 mile wide, in some places less than 700 yards wide.
- *Sea of Marmara:* 130 miles long; 40 miles wide. Turkey maintains the prison island of Imrali, in the sea.
- *The Dardanelles* (the Hellespont of antiquity): 25 miles long; 4 ½ miles wide in the south, 2 ½ miles wide in the north. The Persians invaded ancient Greece by crossing it and during World War I the famous Gallipoli campaign occurred on its shores in 1915.

The treaty that governs the use of the Straits is

THE MONTREUX CONVENTION
JULY 20, 1936

- Restored Turkish sovereignty over the Straits: the Bosporus and Dardanelles, allowing Turkey to remilitarize the zone along the Straits.
- Provided for the free navigation of the Straits by all nations' commercial vessels in peacetime.
- Permitted Turkey to close the Straits to all enemy ships in wartime.

- Specified that Turkey be notified 8 days in advance (or 15 days for non-Black Sea nations' ships) of any ship passing through the Straits.
- Required that ships pass through the Straits singly, unsubmerged, and only in the daytime.

TABLE 7

The Suez Canal historic time-line

DATE	EVENT
1,800-1,200 BCE	Ancient Egyptians built the first version of the Suez Canal.
641 CE	The ancient canal was re-dug by Caliph Omar.
1798	Napoleon had the area surveyed as a site for a new canal.
1832	Ferdinand de Lesseps, French consul in Egypt, studied the feasibility of constructing a new canal.
1858	The *Compagnie Universelle du Canal de Suez* (Suez Canal Company) was formed by de Lesseps.
April 25, 1859	Construction on the canal began.
November 17, 1869	Official opening of the Suez Canal.
November 25, 1875	The United Kingdom gained a major interest in the Suez Canal.
August 25, 1882	The United Kingdom took control of the canal.
March 2, 1888	The Constantinople Convention guaranteed right of passage of all ships through the Suez Canal during war and peace.
November 14, 1936	The British established a Suez Canal Zone under their military control.

June 13, 1956	Last British forces were evacuated and canal zone reverted to Egyptian control.
July 26, 1956	Egyptian President Gamal Abdel Nasser nationalized the Canal.
November 5, 1956-April 8, 1957	Sinai-Suez War; Nasser blocked the canal to international shipping; canal closed.
June 5, 1967-April 10, 1975	Six Day War; Egypt again blocked the canal, which remained closed for almost eight years.

Four wars have been fought over and along the canal: 1956–Sinai-Suez War; 1967–Six Day War; 1967-1970–1000 Day War of Attrition; 1973–Yom Kippur War.

TABLE 8

Sailing distance with and without the use of the Suez Canal

FROM/TO	NO SUEZ CANAL	VIA THE SUEZ CANAL
London, United Kingdom to the Persian Gulf	11,310 miles	6,537 miles
Naples, Italy to Massawa, Eritrea	10,850 miles	2,178 miles
Rotterdam, the Netherlands to Tokyo, Japan	15,045 miles	11,302

THE STRAIT OF TIRAN

The entrance to the Gulf of Aqaba (Eilat) is the narrow Enterprise Passage, a shipping channel only 1,300 yards wide. Two wars were triggered by Egyptian blockade of the Strait of Tiran: The 1956 Sinai-Suez War and the 1967 Six Day War.

BAB EL-MANDEB

The Bab el-Mandeb, ("Gate of Tears") controls the southern approaches to the Red Sea. Perim Island sits in the strait, dividing it into a smaller strait 1 ¾ miles wide, and a larger strait, 9 miles wide. The Arabs imposed a blockade on this international waterway during the 1973 Yom Kippur War.

STRAIT OF HORMUZ

The Strait of Hormuz is the body of water that connects the Persian Gulf to the Gulf of Oman and the Arabian Sea beyond. It is 28 miles wide and 170 miles long. Territorially, it is flanked by Iran to the north and Oman's 51 mile-long enclave, Ruus al Jibal, on the Ras Mussandam Peninsula, to the south.

Both Iran and Oman claim 12 mile-wide limits thus leaving a four mile-wide slot of international waters. Within that four mile-wide area are two shipping lanes, each one mile wide–one northbound, the other southbound, separated by a two mile buffer.

Before the Iran-Iraq War, 1980-1988, an oil-tanker used to pass through the Strait every 10-15 minutes. Currently, during a 24 hour-period, an average 30 vessels transit the strait loaded with roughly 28% of the world's oil consumption—some 17 million barrels of oil per day. This volume varies according to weather conditions, currents, and whether it is day or night. The traffic during the navigable hours tends to be heavy, no more than 6 minutes between each vessel. It is on this vital waterway then that the US receives 12% of its oil and Western Europe and Japan get 25 to 66% of their oil respectively.

A territorial dispute exists between the UAE and Iran over ownership of three islands—Abu Musa, Greater Tunb Island, and Lesser Tunb Island—all strategically located at the mouth of the Strait of Hormuz. In November 1971, Iran forcibly occupied Abu Musa and the Tunbs. The three islands were effectively occupied by Iranian troops in 1992. In 1995, the Iranian Foreign Ministry claimed that the islands were "an inseparable part of Iran." Iran rejected a 1996 proposal by the Gulf Cooperation Council (GCC) for the dispute to be resolved by the International Court of Justice, an option supported by the United Arab Emirates (UAE). On December 31, 2001, the GCC issued a statement reiterating its support for the UAE's sovereignty over Abu Musa and the Tunbs, declared Iran's claims on the islands as "null and void," and backed "all measures...by the UAE to regain sovereignty on its three islands peacefully."

Oman and the UAE are supported by the United States, which guarantees their security (U.S.-Oman Defense agreement 1980) by keeping a naval carrier task force in the Persian Gulf area.

Appendix 2
Etymological History of the Terms "Near East" and "Middle East"

The Roman Empire started the East-West division of the Western world. For many years "the Eastern Question" related to Western dealing with the Ottoman Empire. During the 1890s the Sino-Japanese War of 1894-1895, the division of China into spheres of influence, and the massacres of Armenians, Assyrians, Greeks, and other troubles within the Ottoman Empire forced the creation of two "Eastern Questions"–"Far" and "Near." By 1896, "Near East" was widely used to describe the Middle East.

In 1902, Dr. D.G. Hogarth, a British archeologist and traveler, published *The Near East,* a book about the geography of the region, which helped fix the term and define its limits. He included Albania, Montenegro, southern Serbia (today's Kosovo), Bulgaria, Greece, Egypt, the Ottoman lands of Asia, the Arabian Peninsula, and most of modern Iran up to the area between the Caspian Sea and Indian Ocean.

In September 1902, Captain Alfred Thayer Mahan, author of the authoritative *The Influence of Sea Power upon History (1890)* wrote in *National Review,* an article entitled: "The Persian Gulf and International Relations." In it Mahan first used the term "Middle East." He wrote: "The Middle East if I may adopt a term which I have not seen…" However Mahan did not specify its boundaries.

On October 12, 1902, the ***Times*** of London, ran an article by Valentine Chirol using Mahan's term and helped popularize it, but distinguished Middle East from the Near East and Far East. In Chirol's view, the Near East centered on Turkey, the Middle East centered on India, and the Far East centered on China. After World War I, the definition of Middle East expanded to include areas previously defined as being in the Near East.

Winston Churchill, then Secretary of State for Colonies, established the Colonial Office, Middle Eastern Department to supervise Palestine, Trans-Jordan and Iraq. He was supported by the Royal Geographic Society which declared that the Middle East extended from the Bosporus to the eastern frontiers of India. Near East denoted the Balkans.

During World War II, the British Army had a Middle East Command centered in Cairo, which included Ethiopia, the Somalilands, Eritrea, Libya, Greece, Crete, Iraq, and Iran but still was vague. During the war, Prime Minister Churchill sometimes referred to the Arab areas as the Near East.

After World War II, Churchill wrote: "I had always felt that the name 'Middle East' for Egypt, the Levant, Syria and Turkey, was ill-chosen. This was the Near East. Persia and Iraq were the Middle East, India, Burma and Malaya–the East; and China and Japan the Far East." This was confusing as the Levant had always included Syria, but Churchill listed them separately.

Clement Attlee, who succeeded Churchill, took a slightly different approach declaring: "It has become the accepted practice to use the term 'Middle East' to cover the Arab world and certain neighboring countries. The practice seems to me convenient and I see no reason to change it."

In the March-April 1946 issue of *Geographical Journal,* Attlee was asked about his definition of the term. He remained determined to use "Middle East," but gave a different definition: "… at least the area of Egypt, Palestine, Cyrenaica, Syria and Lebanon, Trans-Jordan, Iraq and the Arabian Peninsula, as well as, in most cases, Persia and Turkey.…"

In 1945, the United Nations assuming that the term "Near East" was dead, listed as its member states in the Middle East: Afghanistan, Iran, Iraq, Syria, Lebanon, Turkey, Saudi Arabia, Yemen, Egypt, Ethiopia, and Greece.

On November 1, 1956, in the midst of the Sinai-Suez War, the *New York Times* stated: "The Middle East is now used in preference to Near East to conform to the change in general usage." In 1957, U.S. Secretary of State John Foster Dulles weighed in with his definition: The Middle East is "the area lying between and including Libya on the west, Pakistan on the east, and Turkey on the north, and the Arabian Peninsula to the south." ". . . I think it should also include

Ethiopia and the Sudan, which lie in Africa, but of which considerable parts lie north of the southern portion of the Arabian Peninsula." In Dulles' view "Middle East" and "Near East" were identical. The 1957 Eisenhower Doctrine (See Appendix 3–Eisenhower Doctrine) passed both Houses of Congress with this definition.

On August 14, 1958, after U.S. forces landed in Lebanon to support its government against United Arab Republic (Egypt and Syria) subversion, the *New York Times* quoted President Dwight D. Eisenhower using the term "Near East." The State Department quickly clarified the "Middle East" and "Near East" as interchangeable for Egypt, Syria, Israel, Jordan, Lebanon, Iraq, Saudi Arabia, and the Persian Gulf sheikhdoms.

In late 1958, the State Department set up its "Aegean and Middle East Division" to cover Greece, Turkey, Cyprus, Iran, Afghanistan, and Pakistan. But if Greece and Turkey are "Aegean" then the rest are the Middle East. All Arab states and Israel were omitted from this division, probably to leave the Soviet Union wondering what was, and what was not covered by the Eisenhower Doctrine.

Currently the State Department has a Bureau of Near East Affairs dealing with Algeria, Bahrain, Egypt, Iran, Iraq, Israel, Jordan, Kuwait, Lebanon, Libya, Morocco, Oman, Qatar, Saudi Arabia, Syria, Tunisia, United Arab Emirates, and Yemen. Similarly, the American Israel Public Affairs Committee (AIPAC) for over half a century has published a bi-weekly newsletter called the "Near East Report."

However, the Middle East Institute in Washington, D.C. defines the Middle East as southwestern Asia and northeastern Africa, from

Mauritania and Morocco to Pakistan, including the Caucasus and Central Asian republics of Kazakhstan, Kyrgyzstan, Uzbekistan, Turkmenistan, and Tajikistan.

Appendix 3
THE EISENHOWER DOCTRINE

H.J. Res. 117–JOINT RESOLUTION TO PROMOTE PEACE AND STABILITY IN THE MIDDLE EAST
March 9, 1957
(Annotated)

"RESOLVED...

That the President be and hereby is authorized to cooperate with and assist any nation or group of nations in the general area of the Middle East desiring such assistance in the development of economic strength dedicated to the maintenance of national independence...

Section 2: The president is authorized to undertake . . . military assistance programs, with any nation or group of nations of that area desiring such assistance . . . if the President determines the necessity thereof, the United States is prepared to use armed forces to assist any such nation or group of such nations requesting assistance against armed aggression from any country controlled by international communism . . ."

Public Law 7, 85th Congress

The president was formally empowered to extend economic and military aid to the nations of the Middle East, provided that they desired it and was threatened by aggression from a communist-controlled country.

The doctrine had two fundamental weaknesses:

1) The main threat to peace and American interests in the Middle East at the time, was not open communist aggression, but the subversion of existing governments.

2) The doctrine could not be put into operation unless some government asked specifically for help

The doctrine was utilized to assist the government of Lebanon in 1958 when it faced subversion by the United Arab Republic (UAR). Since the UAR was a client state of the Soviet Union the terms of the Eisenhower Doctrine were stretched to meet the contingency.

Appendix 4
A Short History of Israel

TABLE 9
A Short History of Israel

DATE	EVENT
c. 1250 BCE	An independent nation of Israel existed in the Land of Israel.
c. 1209	Israel was a known nation according to the Egyptian Mernephtah "Israel" stela.
c.1250-1050	Period of the Judges.
c. 1190	Philistines invaded and took over the southern coast of Canaan.
c. 1050	Philistines captured the Ark of the Covenant.
c. 1025	Saul anointed first king of Israel; fought Philistines and regained some territory.
c. 1010-968	Rule of King David who expelled the Philistines, expanded the Kingdom of Israel, established Jerusalem as its capital, and brought to it the Ark of the Covenant.
968-928	Kingdom of Solomon—First Temple erected; it was Israel's most prosperous and powerful period.
928	Solomon died. Kingdom split into Israel, with its capital at Shchem, and Judah, with its capital at Jerusalem.

878	King Omri of Israel founded new capital at Samaria.
842	Queen Jezebel of Israel imposed cult of Baal and the people revolted. Weakened by internal turmoil, Israel lost land to the Aramaeans.
c. 750	Prophets Amos and Hosea decried exploitation of the poor by the wealthy of Israel.
738	Assyria exacted heavy tribute from Israel.
722	Assyrians invaded the Kingdom of Israel–Samaria destroyed; the Ten Tribes were deported and exiled. Judah became a vassal state under the Assyrians and was forced to pay tribute.
716-687	Hezekiah assumed the throne of Judah, purified religion of Assyrian influences.
701	Assyria besieged Judah.
687	Assyrians besieged Jerusalem.
687-642	Rule of King Manasseh.
639-609	King Josiah of Judah won some territory from Assyria, whose power was declining.
598	Chaldeans (New Babylonians) invaded Judah.
Mar. 16, 597	Chaldeans captured Jerusalem and deported King Jehoiachin.
597-586	Rule of King Zedekiah.
588	Second Chaldean invasion of Judah.
July 18, 586	Jerusalem fell to Nebuchadnezzar II; First Temple destroyed; collapse of the Kingdom of Judah, and its inhabitants were exiled.
Oct. 17, 539	Persian King Cyrus the Great allowed Zerubavel and more than 40,000 Jews to leave Babylon and return to the Land of Israel.
520	The (Second) Temple reconstruction was started.
515	The Second Temple was completed.
445	Ezra read the Torah to the Jews in Jerusalem.

332	Alexander the Great overran the country on his way east.
167-160	Antiochus tried to impose Greek culture; revolt of the Hasmoneans—the Maccabees.
63	Roman General Pompey conquered the region.
37 BCE	Herod renovated and expanded the Second Temple.
30 CE	Jesus was crucified in Jerusalem.
Aug. 11, 70	Jerusalem fell to the Romans; the Second Temple was destroyed.
Apr. 16, 73	Masada fell to the Romans; the Diaspora began a 1,875 year quest to regain Jewish sovereignty and independence.
132-135	The Bar Kokhba rebellion marked the end of autonomous or independent Jewish government.
330-638	Byzantine Christian rule.
614-628	Persian invasion and rule.
637-1071	Arabs invaded from the desert–Arab/Muslim rule.
1071-1099	Seljuk rule.
1099-1187	Crusader Kingdom of Jerusalem.
1187-1250	Ayyubid rule.
1250-1517	Mamelukes from the south invaded and ruled.
1517-1917	Ottoman Turks from the north invaded and ruled.
1870	Mikveh Yisrael—first agricultural settlement began.
1882	First Aliyah—ingathering of the exiles.
1897	Theodor Herzl expounded his vision of a "Jewish State"—the start of modern Zionism.
1905	Second Aliyah—ingathering of the exiles.
1917	Arab riots; Jewish self-defense organized in Jerusalem.
1917-1948	British Mandate over Palestine.

Mar. 1-Apr. 25, 1920	Arab misojudaic attacks against eight Jewish towns including Degania and Rosh Pina. Four other towns had to be abandoned.
1921	Arab misojudaic attacks on six main Jewish towns including Jerusalem, Rehovot, and Petah Tikva.
Aug. 23-26, 1929	Arab misojudaic riots in Jerusalem, Safed, and other towns; massacre in Hebron. Seven Jewish communities abandoned.
1936-1939	Arab riots - organized Arab gangs; Jewish covert and overt defense force forged.
1939-1947	Struggle and revolt of Jewish Underground against British rule.
Nov. 29, 1947	United Nations General Assembly adopted Resolution 181 calling for creation of a Jewish State.
1947-1949	First Arab war against Israel—Israeli War of Independence.
May 14, 1948	Re-establishment of Jewish sovereignty over the ancient Jewish homeland as the State of Israel was proclaimed.
1948-1967	Jordanians invaded and ruled Judea-Samaria (what the Arabs called the "West Bank") and Old City of Jerusalem.
Nov. 7, 1956	The Sinai-Suez War.
June 5-10, 1967	Third Arab war against Israel–the Six Day War.
June 7, 1967	Jerusalem reunited under Israeli control.
Sept. 1967-Aug. 7, 1970	Fourth Arab war against Israel–the 1000 Day War of Attrition.
Oct. 6-26, 1973	Fifth Arab war against Israel–the Yom Kippur War.
Mar. 26, 1979	Israel-Egypt Peace Treaty.
June 7, 1981	Israeli air strike on Iraqi nuclear facility at Osirak.

June 6, 1982-Sept. 1982	Sixth Arab war against Israel–the Israel-PLO war in Lebanon.
Dec. 6, 1987-1993	Palestinian Arab *intifada* uprising and terrorism.
Jan.-Feb. 1991	Israel bombed by Iraqi missiles during Gulf War I.
Sept. 13, 1993	Israel-Palestine Liberation Organization Oslo agreement.
Oct. 26, 1994	Israel-Jordan Peace Treaty.
Sept. 28, 1995	Israel-Palestinian Oslo 2 or Taba Interim agreement.
Oct. 23, 1998	Israel-Palestinian Wye River Memorandum.
July 11-25, 2000	Camp David II Summit to reach a final status settlement–rejected by the Palestinian Arabs.
Sept. 28, 2000-2005	Palestinian Arab Al Aqsa Intifada uprising and continued terrorism including suicide bombings.
June 25– Aug. 14, 2006	Seventh Arab-Muslim war against Israel—the Second Lebanon (Hezbollah) War.
Sept. 6, 2007	Israeli air strike on Syrian nuclear weapons facility.

Appendix 5

Population Exchanges and Transfers

Transfers and population exchanges have been a solution for many intractable problems in 20th century history. After World War I and II, transferring populations was considered legal and moral, and the most favored response to inter-ethnic strife. The first population-exchanges involved Bulgaria, Greece, and Turkey. The Treaty of Neuilly of November 27, 1919, provided for 46,000 Greeks from Bulgaria and 96,000 Bulgarians from Greece to switch countries.

After the defeat of the Greek army in the Greek-Turkish War of 1921-1922, and the Turkish assault against Greek communities in Turkey, Greek refugees began fleeing their homes in Turkey. Greece and Turkey voluntarily exchanged populations with about 1.2 million Greeks, who were Turkish citizens, and about 500,000 Turks, who were Greek citizens. The Greeks were absorbed by Greece.

In 1937, the Peel Commission in British Mandatory Palestine, concluded, "An irrepressible conflict has arisen between two national communities within the narrow bounds of one small country. There is no common ground between them. Their national aspirations are incompatible... Neither of the two national ideals permits of combination in the service of a single State."

If partition is to succeed, the Commission said, drawing new boundaries and establishing two separate states will not be sufficient. "Sooner or later there should be a transfer of land, and as far as possible, an exchange of population."

A number of leading Zionist leaders favored such ideas, as did Presidents Herbert Hoover and Franklin Roosevelt, Czechoslovakian President Edvard Beneš, and three Nobel Peace Prize winners: Sir Norman Angell, Christian Lange, and Philip Noel-Baker. However, due to outright Arab rejection of the Peel Commission report, the continuing Arab Revolt of 1936-1939, and the rapid approach of World War II, nothing was done.

On September 7, 1940, the Treaty of Craiova, recognized by the major European powers, returned Southern Dobruja to Bulgaria. It had been under Romanian control. As a result, population exchange occurred, whereby 80,000 Romanians left Southern Dobruja and were resettled in Romania, and 65,000 Bulgarians from Romanian Northern Dobruja moved to Bulgaria.

Sometimes such transfer/exchange is the result of conflict. After World War II, 15 million Germans were transferred from Poland, Czechoslovakia, Hungary, the Soviet Union, and East Germany to West Germany. After the borders in Europe were redrawn, smaller transfers were made in parts of Central and Eastern Europe.

In Asia, at the conclusion of World War II, 6.289 million Japanese were transferred from their former empire in Manchuria, Korea, China, and Southeast Asia.

Population transfer was also used to settle the inter-religious enmity between Hindus and Muslims in British India in 1947. Once it became clear the communities could not live together, the sub-continent was partitioned into two states–India and Pakistan. This required the resettlement of some 15 million people. 7.5 million Muslims left India in 1947 –that is 10 times the number of Arabs who left Israel in 1947-1949. Similarly, 7.5 million Hindus and Sikhs were forced out of Pakistan.

After Turkey invaded and occupied the northern part of Cyprus in July 1974, more than 200,000 Cypriots fled or were relocated across the Attila Line–also known as the "Green Line"–set up by the Turkish military. Greek-Cypriots left the Turkish-occupied zone, while Turkish Cypriots escaped to the north, where they moved into homes abandoned by Greek-Cypriots. The Greek-Cypriot refugees resettled in the southern part of the island, a number on property owned by Turkish-Cypriots. The right to recover property and the right to return are two of the key obstacles to settling this dispute. While Turkey was criticized for the large numbers of Greek and Turkish Cypriots who were displaced, the transfer of Greeks and Turks was completed and the de facto partition of Cyprus remains to this day, without international condemnation.

After the disintegration of the Soviet Union in 1991, there would be a population exchange of thousands among the Caucasus areas of Armenia, Nagorno-Karabakh, Azerbaijan, Abkhazia, South Ossetia, and Georgia.

Why did these transfers take place? One main reason is because the two groups involved could not live in peace with one another.

That has been the case between Israel and its Arab/Muslim neighbors all along.

The Palestinian Arabs already have a state called Jordan, where they make up some 80% of the population on over 77% of the original Mandate of Palestine's territory (See Appendix 6–Mandatory Palestine Land Facts). Those who live in Judea-Samaria (what the Arabs call the "West Bank") and Gaza overwhelmingly do not want to have Jews in their midst, overwhelmingly favor the continued use of terror and violence to kill Jews, and wish to destroy Israel. No number of negotiations, or agreements, including the so-called Oslo "peace process," changes that fact.

Appendix 6
Mandatory Palestine Land Facts

On April 25, 1920, the San Remo conference passed a resolution which recognized Great Britain's mandate in Palestine to encompass what are now Jordan, Israel, the Golan Heights, Judea and Samaria (what the Arabs call the "West Bank"), and the Gaza Strip. The conference also affirmed Britain's 1917 Balfour Declaration (See Appendix 7–The Balfour Declaration), favoring a "national home" in Palestine for the Jewish people. It incorporated Article 22 of the Covenant of the League of Nations and was the basic document upon which the Mandate for Palestine was constructed.

While the decision made at San Remo created the Palestine Mandate *de facto*, the mandate document signed by Great Britain as the Mandatory and the League of Nations made it *de jure.* It thus became a binding treaty in international law. The resolution of the League of Nations creating the Palestine Mandate included the following significant statement:

"Whereas recognition has thereby been given to the historical connection of the Jewish people with Palestine and to the grounds for reconstituting their national home in that country; . . ." This move was unique in history. No such recognition had ever been accorded to anyone, ever. Palestine was to be held for the Jewish people wherever they lived.

"ARTICLE 2 The Mandatory shall be responsible for placing the country under such political, administrative and economic conditions as will secure the establishment of the Jewish national home, as laid down in the preamble, and the development of self-governing institutions, and also for safeguarding the civil and religious rights of all the inhabitants of Palestine, irrespective of race and religion."

Thus the operative clause specifically referred to the preamble and reiterated that there were no political rights for other inhabitants.

"ARTICLE 5 The Mandatory shall be responsible for seeing that no Palestine territory shall be ceded or leased to, or in any way placed under the control of the Government of any foreign Power."

"ARTICLE 6 The Administration of Palestine, while ensuring that the rights and position of other sections of the population are not prejudiced, shall facilitate Jewish immigration under suitable conditions and shall encourage, in co-operation with the Jewish agency referred to in Article 4, close settlement by Jews on the land, including State lands and waste lands not required for public purposes."

In 1921, Great Britain, bowing to Arab pressure, closed the area east of the Jordan River to Jewish settlement–but not the area west of it to accelerating Arab migration. Great Britain--its mandate now confirmed by the League of Nations--unilaterally created Trans-Jordan on 77.5 percent of the original mandate land.

In reaction to Arab violence in Palestine in 1920 and 1921, the British took steps to prevent the Jews from establishing a state on the remainder (22.5%) of the land. They blocked Jewish immigration and limited the right of Jews to purchase and settle the land to a tiny portion of the territory.

In 1923, Great Britain transferred the Golan Heights to the French mandate for Syria. This being the case, Israel in 1949 ended up with 17.5 percent of mandate Palestine. Judea-Samaria (what the Arabs call the "West Bank") and Gaza Strip are the remaining unallocated, disputed 5 percent.

It should be emphasized that Mandatory Palestine has already been partitioned into two states, one Arab and one Jewish, Jordan and Israel, respectively. Now there is the call for a second Arab Palestinian state (See Appendix 8–A Second Palestinian State?). Whatever the apportionment of the final 5 percent, Israel does not and will not have a majority of the land.

After World War II, in 1945, the United Nations succeeded the League of Nations and assumed its responsibilities. The new United Nations Charter included the following:

"ARTICLE 80 . . . nothing in this Charter shall be construed in or of itself to alter in any manner the rights whatsoever of any states or any peoples or the terms of existing international instruments to which Members of the United Nations may respectively be parties." Thus the Mandate of Palestine continued without change.

Appendix 7
The Balfour Declaration

Foreign Office, November 2nd, 1917

Dear Lord Rothschild,

I have much pleasure in conveying to you, on behalf of His Majesty's Government, the following declaration of sympathy with Jewish Zionist aspirations which has been submitted to, and approved by, the Cabinet.

"His Majesty's Government view with favour *the establishment in Palestine of a national home for the Jewish people,* and will use their best endeavors to facilitate the achievement of this object, it being clearly understood that *nothing shall be done which may prejudice the civil and religious rights of existing non-Jewish communities in Palestine,* or the rights and political status enjoyed by Jews in any other country. (**Emphasis added**)"

I should be grateful if you would bring this declaration to the knowledge of the Zionist Federation.

Yours,
Arthur James Balfour
British Foreign Secretary

The Balfour Declaration was a deliberate act of the British Cabinet, part of their general foreign policy and aims in World War I. It was invested with international status when Russia, France, Italy, and the United States all gave their consent to it, in advance.

The Balfour Declaration does not treat the Jews and the non-Jews mentioned, on an equal basis. The Jews were referred to in connection with regard to their "Zionist aspirations" and their "national home." The non-Jews referred to as "the existing non-Jewish communities," were entitled to enjoy "civil and religious rights"–not political ones. Arab national aspirations were recognized outside of British Mandatory Palestine.

APPENDIX 8
A SECOND PALESTINIAN STATE?

(Adapted by the author from his article *"THE RIGHT QUESTION: ARE THE PALESTINIAN ARABS DESERVING OF A SECOND STATE?* Dec. 26, 2005 - featured on the internet at Think-Israel.org, Dec. 29, 2005)

Must all national and ethnic groups that want their own states and have struggled for them get them, in the name of self-determination? If so, why is there no state of Tibet; Lunda state of Katanga; Luba state of South Kasai; Ibo state of Biafra; Azania state of Southern Sudan; Tamil state in Sri Lanka; and a state of Kurdistan?

Of all the peoples on earth who have not yet been granted the sovereignty they have fought for—the Chechens of Russia, the Uighurs of China, the Karens of Myanmar, the Mizos and Nagas of northeast India, the Saharawis of Morocco, and the Acehans of Indonesia, to name but a few—why must the Palestinian Arabs be given a second Palestinian Arab state? They already make up some 80% of the population of Jordan, a nation created by the British in 1921 from over 77% of the original British Mandate of Palestine which was to be the Jewish National homeland.

Should the Palestinian Arabs alone be acknowledged by many of deserving not one but two states? Thus far the historic record has shown a lack of Palestinian Arab ability to govern and police themselves. Recall that the Palestinian Authority has in effect governed Gaza since 1994, save for the 21 Jewish communities located there and subsequently evicted by the Israeli government.

One important benchmark of nationhood must be the degree of difference from its neighbors, and the need for a state to protect that uniqueness. The Tibetans, for example, have their own special culture, language, and religion, which they will lose if they continue to be ruled by the Chinese; the Kurds have a culture and language unlike that of the Arabs; the Karens a language and religion different from that of the Burmese.

But the Palestinian Arabs of Judea, Samaria (what the Arabs call the "West Bank") and Gaza, speak the same dialect of Arabic, share the same Islamic faith, have the same family structure, customs, dress, food, music and social values as is found in Jordan and Syria. Indeed, many have strong family ties to Palestinian Arabs in Jordan and share a common border with the Arabs of Jordan. Furthermore, they live in an environment whose physical landscape, flora, fauna, and climate are indistinguishable from much of Jordan and Syria.

The international community, nevertheless, expects all the aforementioned peoples to get along with the nations of which they are a part–the Chechens with Russia, the Tibetans with China, the Western Saharans with Morocco, as well as the others. Why not the Palestinian Arabs? Why give them now, a second state? The answer is simple: Arab pressure and global appeasement and capitulation. The Arab people already have self-determination as expressed in 21 sovereign countries (See Appendix 9-A territorial comparison). Is there a need for a 22nd Arab state–a second Palestinian state?

APPENDIX 9
A TERRITORIAL COMPARISON

The 21 Arab states have a total area of 5,311,458 sq. miles, which is slightly less than 1 ½ times the size of the 50 United States (3,794,085 sq. miles).

Israel's area is 8,019 sq. miles, smaller than the State of New Jersey (8,721 sq. miles). The ratio of Arab to Jewish land is over 640:1. Syria alone is seven times the size of Israel (71,498 sq. miles). Texas is 267,339 sq. miles. Israel can fit into Texas over 33 times (33.33). Arizona is 113,642 sq. miles. Israel can fit into Arizona over 14 times (14.17). Forty-five American states are larger than Israel. Lake Erie is larger than Israel and Lake Michigan more than twice as large. If Israel were dropped into Lake Michigan it would disappear from view without a trace.

Israel is about the size of Maricopa County, Arizona. It is less than one-half the size of San Bernardino County, California. Israel including Judea-Samaria, Gaza, and Golan is 10,846 sq. miles. Gaza is 139 sq. miles. Judea-Samaria (what the Arabs call the "West Bank") is 2,263 sq. miles. The Golan Heights is 451 sq. miles. The distance from Israel's capital in Jerusalem to Bethlehem in the Palestinian territory is only a fraction of the distance from Washington, D.C., to Baltimore, Maryland.

Appendix 10
The Palestinian National Covenant

(Annotated)

Israel is the only nation in the world for which a warrant for destruction exists in writing–the Palestinian National Covenant.

The Palestinian National Covenant was adopted on May 28, 1964. After the Six Day War of June 1967, it was revised into its current form on July 17, 1968, during a meeting of the Palestine National Council.

It should be noted that Article 24 of the Palestine Liberation Organization's (PLO) original founding document, states: "this Organization [the PLO] does not exercise any regional sovereignty over the West Bank in the Hashemite Kingdom of Jordan, in the Gaza Strip or the Himmah area." For the PLO before the Six-Day War of 1967, Palestine was Israel. It was not Judea-Samaria (what the Arabs call the "West Bank") or the Gaza Strip. Those areas, during the period 1949-1967, were under the occupation of other Arab states–Egypt and Jordan. The only "homeland" for the PLO in

1964 was the State of Israel. However, in response to the Six Day War, the PLO revised its Covenant on July 17, 1968, to remove the operative language of Article 24, thereby newly asserting a Palestinian claim of sovereignty to Judea-Samaria (what the Arabs call the "West Bank") and the Gaza Strip.

Zahir Muhse'in, a member of the PLO Executive Committee, in a March 31, 1977, interview with the Amsterdam-based newspaper *Trouw*, revealed the change in territorial aspirations to include not only Israel but Judea-Samaria (what the Arabs call the "West Bank") and the Gaza Strip. In doing this the PLO admitted the fact that the Palestinian people were in fact a PLO invention:

"The Palestinian people do not exist. The creation of a Palestinian state is only a means for continuing our struggle against the state of Israel for our Arab unity. In reality today there is no difference between Jordanians, Palestinian Arabs, Syrians and Lebanese. Only for political and tactical reasons do we speak today about the existence of a Palestinian people, since Arab national interests demand that we posit the existence of a distinct "Palestinian people" to oppose Zionism. For tactical reasons, Jordan, which is a sovereign state with defined borders, cannot raise claims to Haifa and Jaffa, while as a Palestinian, I can undoubtedly demand Haifa, Jaffa, Beer-Sheva and Jerusalem. However, the moment we reclaim our right to all of Palestine, we will not wait even a minute to unite Palestine and Jordan."

The word "covenant" is used to emphasize the sanctity of the document.

A total of 30 of the 33 articles in the Covenant effectively deny Israel's right to exist as a Jewish state. They call for the demise of Israel either explicitly or implicitly,

Articles 15, 19, 20, 22, and 23 of the Covenant explicitly deny Israel's right to exist as a Jewish state. Articles 1-6, 8, 11-14, 16-18, 21, 24-26, 28, and 29 implicitly deny the State of Israel's right to exist. These articles recognize that Palestinian Arabs have the sole right to all of the land. Articles 7, 9, and 10 call all Arabs to support an armed struggle against the State of Israel. Articles 27 and 30 indirectly call for violence.

- "ARTICLE 1: Palestine will be an Arab State [this belies the claim that Palestine will be a secular, democratic state. 13 Arab states' constitutions proclaim Islam as the religion of the state].
- ARTICLE 2: Boundaries…as at the time of the British Mandate… one integral unit, [No separate Jewish state. It has been repeatedly stressed that the *Falastin (Palestine)* that the PLO seeks to create will extend *min al-nahr ila al bahr* (from the river to the sea)].
- ARTICLE 3: Only Palestinian Arabs possess legal right to self-determination, not the Jews. [Thus it is more important for the Arabs to have a 22nd Arab state, than for the Jews to have one Jewish state].
- ARTICLE 6: Jews who lived in Palestine before the "Zionist invasion" will be allowed to remain [At first this was defined as 1917, but in the United Nations General Assembly on Nov. 13, 1974, Yasir Arafat stated "the Jewish invasion began… in 1881" All others would have to go, one way or another].

- ARTICLE 9: Armed struggle is the only way to liberate Palestine [Thus negotiations, cease-fires, *hudnas*, peace processes, and road maps–are all tactics to culminate in the politicide of Israel].
- ARTICLE 15: [We call for] the liquidation of the Zionist presence in Palestine.
- ARTICLE 19: The UN Partition plan of 1947 and the establishment of Israel is fundamentally null and void, whatever time has elapsed ..." [This reiterates the rejection of Jewish self-determination. The UN Partition plan was voided by invading Arab armies in 1948].
- ARTICLE 20: ...nor do Jews constitute a single nation [Thus denies the existence of the Jewish people as a nation and any ties that it might have to the Land of Israel].
- ARTICLE 22: The liberation of Palestine will destroy the Zionist and imperialist presence and will contribute to the establishment of peace in the Middle East ...
- ARTICLE 27: The PLO will cooperate with all Arab States and will not interfere in the internal affairs of any Arab state [Yet they tried to overthrow the Jordanian monarchy and take over that nation in 1970, and plunged Lebanon into civil war in 1975].
- ARTICLE 29: Legitimizes PLO terror attacks on any countries that are friendly to Israel."

The bottom line is that the Palestinian National Covenant calls for the destruction of the State of Israel. The Israelis, quite naturally, thought that the inflammatory language should be changed before they could consider the PLO to be a serious "partner for peace".

The Covenant specifically states, in Article 33, that there can be no changes without the express decision of the Palestine National Council.

What did Yasir Arafat agree to do?

In a letter to Israeli Prime Minister Yitzhak Rabin, dated September 9, 1993—part of the Oslo Accords—signed by Yasir Arafat as Chairman of the PLO and Fatah leader, Arafat agreed that:

- "... the PLO renounces the use of terrorism and other acts of violence and will assume responsibility over all PLO elements and personnel in order to assure their compliance, prevent violations and discipline violators.
- ... those articles of the Palestinian Covenant which deny Israel's right to exist, and the provisions of the Covenant which are inconsistent with the commitments of this letter are now inoperative and no longer valid.
- ... the PLO undertakes to submit to the Palestinian National Council for formal approval the necessary changes in regard to the Palestinian Covenant."

But nothing was done to change the Covenant. The requirement was restated in another letter from Arafat to Rabin which accompanied the May 4, 1994 Agreement on the Gaza Strip and Jericho Area (the Cairo Agreement), but no action was taken by Arafat and the PLO. Because the changes were not made, the 1995 Israeli-Palestinian Interim Agreement (Oslo II) made the requirement even more specific:

- "ARTICLE XXXI (9): The PLO undertakes that, within two months of the date of the inauguration of the Council, the

Palestinian National Council will convene and formally approve the necessary changes in regard to the Palestinian Covenant, as undertaken in the letters signed by the Chairman of the PLO and addressed to the Prime Minister of Israel, dated September 9, 1993 and May 4, 1994."

What actions were taken by the PLO to live up to its agreements?

The Oslo II agreement was signed on September 24, 1995 but the change was not made within the time period specified. On April 24, 1996 there was a vote by the PLO's Palestine National Council, meeting in Gaza. They issued a statement saying that it had become aged, and that an undefined part of it would be rewritten at an undetermined date in the future.

While the English language press release stated that the PLO Covenant was "hereby amended," the Arabic version of Yasir Arafat's letter on this declaration stated:

"It has been decided upon:

1. Changing the Palestine National Charter by canceling the articles that are contrary to the letters exchanged between the PLO and the Government of Israel, on September 9 and 10, 1993.

2. The PNC will appoint a legal committee with the task of redrafting the National Charter. The Charter will be presented to the first meeting of the Central Council."

The governments of the United States and of Israel welcomed the vote, stating that it marked the fulfillment of the Palestinian obligation on the Covenant. But, again, that was not actually the case. The PNC action, which has not been officially fully disclosed, only stated an intention to make changes at a future date and did not specify, in detail, the changes that would be made. The matter was referred to a legal committee for study. No specific anti-Israel clauses in the Covenant were declared officially abrogated. Moreover, the process was incomplete because the PNC did not draft a new Covenant.

Peace Watch, a left-wing Israeli peace group that promotes the creation of a Palestinian state, issued this statement, which represents the way most Israelis feel: The decision fails to meet the obligations laid out in the Oslo accords in two respects.

First, the actual amendment of the Covenant has been left for a future date. As of now, the old Covenant, in its original form, remains the governing document of the PLO, and will continue in this status until the amendments are actually approved... There is a sharp difference between calling for something to change and actually implementing the changes.

Second, the decision does not specify which clauses will be amended.

After winning the election in May 1996, Israeli Prime Minister Netanyahu declared the failure to revise the Covenant to be a violation of the agreements by the Palestinian Arabs. In the 1997 Hebron Protocol, it was specifically noted, again, that the PLO was committed to, "Complete the process of revising the Palestinian National Charter." Thereafter, Arafat and the PLO governing bodies insisted that they were in compliance based on the PNC vote in

1996, but legal analysts do not agree. In January 1998, Chairman Arafat sent letters to President Clinton and Prime Minister Tony Blair purporting to "put to rest" concerns about the PNC resolution and setting out a list of articles supposedly canceled or amended by the decision. But personal statements by Arafat have no legal effect; only a vote of 2/3 of the PNC can amend the Covenant (Article 33). On December 14, 1998, the Palestinian National Council, in accordance with the Wye Memorandum, which required compliance with the earlier agreements, convened in Gaza in the presence of US President Clinton and voted to reaffirm their decision to amend the Covenant. But, again, this was insubstantial window dressing. Their action didn't actually amend the Covenant and the Palestinian Authority remained in violation of the lengthening series of agreements.

Although the Palestinian National Council (PNC) has twice taken formal decisions to revise the Palestinian National Covenant (1996 and 1998) calling for Israel's destruction, the PNC Chairman, Salim Za'anoun, stated on February 3, 2001, in the official Palestinian Authority newspaper, **Al-Hayat Al-Jadida,** that the Palestinian Covenant remained unchanged and was still in force [**Al-Hayat Al-Jadida**, 3 February 2001, as translated by MEMRI].

Former CIA Director James Woolsey said:

"Arafat has been like Lucy with the football, treating the rest of the world as Charlie Brown. He and the PNC keep telling everyone they've changed the charter, without actually changing it."

This saga of the Covenant revision is an example of the lack of good faith on the part of Arafat and the Palestinian Arabs in the course of the Oslo peace process. But, it probably does not make a difference whether the Covenant is actually revised or not. The hatred and violence directed against Israel by the Palestinian Arabs does not originate with the piece of paper called the Palestinian National Covenant.

It should be noted that in 1998, Al Fatah published a new constitution that goes beyond the Palestinian National Covenant in calling for the destruction of Israel.

Though changes in the charter were ratified by PLO governing bodies, the original charter is still displayed by the Palestine legation to the UN and other Palestinian bodies. In PNA offices there is a plaque commemorating the original 18 signers of the Charter or Covenant.

ISLAMIC RESISTANCE MOVEMENT- THE HAMAS COVENANT, 1988

(Excerpts)

In its platform Hamas states ". . . Israel will rise and will remain erect until Islam eliminates it as it had eliminated its predecessors."

Introduction - "For our struggle against the Jews is extremely wide-ranging and grave, so much so that it will need all the loyal efforts we can wield, to be followed by further steps and reinforced by successive battalions from the multifarious Arab and Islamic world, until the enemies are defeated and Allah's victory prevails."

ARTICLE 6: "The Islamic Resistance Movement is a distinct Palestinian Movement which owes its loyalty to Allah, derives from Islam its way of life and strives to raise the banner of Allah over every inch of Palestine."

ARTICLE 11: ". . . the land of Palestine has been an Islamic Waqf [trust] throughout the generations and until the Day of Resurrection, no one can renounce it or part of it, or abandon it or part of it."

ARTICLE 13: "[Peace] initiatives, the so-called peaceful solutions, and the international conferences to resolve the Palestinian problem, are all contrary to the beliefs of the Islamic Resistance Movement. For renouncing any part of Palestine means renouncing part of the religion. . . .There is no solution to the Palestinian problem except by Jihad."

ARTICLE 15: "I swear by that who holds in His Hands the Soul of Muhammad! I indeed wish to go to war for the sake of Allah! I will assault and kill, assault and kill, assault and kill *(told by Bukhari and Muslim)*."

ARTICLE 22: The enemies of Hamas established ". . . clandestine organizations which are spreading around the world, in order to destroy societies and carry out Zionist interests. Such organizations are: the Freemasons, Rotary Clubs, Lions Clubs, and B'nai B'rith and the like." Note: Ordinary Western institutions are labeled as enemies of the Islamic Resistance.

ARTICLE 28: "... The Arab states surrounding Israel are required to open their borders to the Jihad fighters, the sons of the Arab and Islamic peoples, to enable them to play their role and to join their efforts to those of their brothers among the Muslim Brothers in Palestine."

Israel, by virtue of its being Jewish and of having a Jewish population, defies Islam and the Muslims.

ARTICLE 33: "...until the Decree of Allah is fulfilled, the ranks are over-swollen, Jihad fighters join other Jihad fighters, and all this accumulation sets out from everywhere in the Islamic world, obeying the call of duty, and intoning 'Come on, join Jihad!' This call will tear apart the clouds in the skies and it will continue to ring until liberation is completed, the invaders are vanquished and Allah's victory sets in."

FATAH CONSTITUTION, 1964
(Excerpts)

ARTICLE 4: "The Palestinian struggle is part and parcel of the world-wide struggle against Zionism, colonialism and international imperialism"

ARTICLE 7: "The Zionist movement is racial, colonial and aggressive in ideology, goals, organization and method."

ARTICLE 8: "The Israeli existence in Palestine is a Zionist invasion with a colonial expansive base, and it is a natural ally to colonialism and international imperialism."

ARTICLE 12: "[The] Complete liberation of Palestine and eradication of Zionist economic, political, military, and cultural existence."

ARTICLE 13: "Establishing an independent democratic state with complete sovereignty on all Palestinian lands, [a *Falestin* (Palestine) that extends *min al-nahr ila al bahr* (from the river to the sea)] and Jerusalem is its capital city, and protecting the citizens' legal and equal rights without any racial or religious discrimination."

ARTICLE 17: "Armed public revolution is the inevitable method to liberating Palestine."

ARTICLE 19: "Armed struggle is a strategy and not a tactic, and the Palestinian Arab People's armed revolution is a decisive factor in the liberation fight and in uprooting the Zionist existence, and this struggle will not cease until the Zionist state is demolished and Palestine is completely liberated."

ARTICLE 22: "Opposing any political solution offered as an alternative to demolishing the Zionist occupation in Palestine."

ARTICLE 23: "Maintaining relations with Arab countries… with the proviso that the armed struggle is not negatively affected".

ARTICLE 24: "Maintaining relations with all liberal forces supporting our just struggle in order to resist together Zionism and imperialism."

ARTICLE 25: "Convincing concerned countries in the world to prevent Jewish immigration to Palestine as a method of solving the problem."

Some have labeled Fatah as "moderate" and Hamas as "extremist." It should be emphasized that both have the same goal, the elimination of Israel. Whereas Fatah (as well as the PLO, al-Aqsa Brigades and other groups under the PLO umbrella) are a crafty, secular, politically-slick, media-savvy group of killers, who give lip service in English to the "peace process;" Hamas (Islamic Jihad, Fatah al-Islam et al) are ideologically-driven, religiously-motivated, fanatically-dedicated murderers. Fatah/PLO negotiates while killing Israelis, whereas Hamas murders Israelis without negotiating.

APPENDIX 11
THE SPREAD OF ISLAM

Islam is the fastest growing religion in the world today. A lot more of the world lives under *Sharia* (Islamic law) than was the case some thirty years ago. To cite the most prominent examples: Pakistan adopted it in 1977; Iran in 1979; and Sudan in 1984. Fifty years ago, Nigeria lived under English common law; now, half of that country is under Islamic law.

Since the beginning of 2005, for example, some 10 percent of southern Thailand's Buddhist population has abandoned their homes, a fact that has largely gone unreported in the Western press. Whatever one's opinion of the various local conflicts around the world — Muslims vs. Buddhists in Thailand, Muslims vs. Catholics in the Philippines, Muslims vs. Hindus in Kashmir, Muslims vs. Jews in the Land of Israel, Muslims vs. Russian Orthodox in Chechnya, Muslims vs. Christians across Africa — the fact is the *jihad* has held out a long time against very tough enemies. If the Islamofascists are not afraid of taking on the Israelis and Russians, why would they fear the Danes, the Swedes, the Dutch, the Belgians, the French, the Spaniards or even the British?

APPENDIX 12
TIME LINE OF ISLAM, MUSLIM CONQUESTS, AND SETBACKS

TABLE 10
Time Line of Islam, Muslim Conquests and Setbacks
(Key events in Islamic history and setbacks are italicized)

DATE	EVENT
570	*Birth of Muhammad.*
610	*Muhammad believed he had a vision and was chosen to serve as the prophet of a new faith.*
622	*The Hegira. Beginning of the Islamic era. (Year 1 A.H. in the Islamic calendar).*
624	Muhammad's first major battle, the Battle of Badr led to victorious entry into Medina.
March 31, 627	*Meccan forces attacked Muhammad in Medina.*
628	*Muhammad signed the Treaty of Al-Hudaybiyya with the Meccans providing for a 10 year truce.*

629	Muslim forces defeated the Jews at the Battle of Khaybar. The imposition of tribute upon the conquered Jews, in the Pact of Khaybar, served as a precedent for provisions in Islamic law requiring the exaction of *jizya*–tribute–from *dhimmis*, i.e. non-Muslims under Muslim rule, and confiscation of land belonging to non-Muslims into the collective property of the *umma*–the Muslim community.
January 630	After only two and a half years, Muhammad conquered Mecca from his base in Medina.
March 632	"I was ordered to fight all men until they say 'There is no god but Allah.'"—Prophet Muhammad's farewell address.
632	*Death of Muhammad in Medina at age 59. Islam controls Hejaz (the western area of the Arabian Peninsula).*
632	*Abu Bakr, Muhammad's father-in-law, became the first Caliph and established the Caliphate (khilaafa, or, "succession").*
633–637	Muslim Arab conquest of Syria and the surrounding lands, all Christian, including present-day Israel, as well as Mesopotamia (present-day Iraq). It marked the beginnings of a great wave of Muslim conquests and the rapid advance of Islam outside Arabia.
634	*Umar became the second Caliph.*
Aug. 20, 636	The Battle of Yarmuk took place in Syria. The Muslim Arabs, led by Khalid bin Walid, defeated Christians of the Byzantine Empire under Heraclius.
636–642	Persia conquered by the Muslims.
637	Battle of Qadisiyya, a Muslim victory over the Sasanian army; Muslim conquest of Mesopotamia.
637–1071	Conquest and occupation of Jerusalem and the Land of Israel.

639	Conquest of Armenia and Khuzistan (southwestern Persia).
639-642	Islamic forces under General Amr ibn al-As invaded the Nile Valley. By 642 all of Egypt was conquered.
643	Conquest of Libya and Azerbaijan.
644	Murder of Umar; Uthman became the third Caliph.
647	Conquest of Cyprus.
651	Conquest of Persia completed.
652-665	Conquest of much of North Africa.
656	*Murder of Uthman. Start of Islamic civil war.*
661	*Murder of Ali, the fourth Caliph. The Umayyad family claimed rule of the Caliphate. These events marked the split between Sunnis and Shiites in Islam.*
662-709	Conquest of Transoxiana (Afghanistan region); Kabul captured in 670; Bukhara became a vassal state in 674.
664-712	Conquest of Sindh (modern day Pakistan and Kashmir).
668	The tenth caliph, Abd al-Malik, began building the Dome of the Rock on the Temple Mount in Jerusalem. It was completed in 691.
672	Muslim forces captured the island of Rhodes.
674-678	First Muslim siege of Constantinople.
October 10, 680	*The Battle of Karbala was fought in present-day Iraq between the forces of Husayn ibn Ali (grandson of the Prophet) and the Umayyads. Husayn's small force, including women and children were wiped out. The event is a central theme of Shi'a Islam.*

681	Muslim forces under General Uqba ibn Nafi reached the Atlantic Ocean after crossing North Africa. Nafi rode his horse into the waves drew his sword and exclaimed: "God of Muhammad! If I heard there was a country beyond these waters, I would go there and carry the glory of your name there as well!"
697	Carthage (in present day Tunisia) was conquered.
700	Muslim forces waged military campaigns against the Berbers in North Africa.
700	*Muslim forces in North Africa, turned southward across the Sahara and attacked the Kingdom of Ghana. They were repulsed.*
700-1606	Conquered Nubia (northern Sudan).
701-705	Invaded and defeated Armenia.
705-827	Numerous attacks on Crete; the island was finally conquered in 827.
April 29, 711	Muslim forces began to expand into Europe from the west as Tariq ibn Ziyad (after whom Gibraltar was named: the Rock of Tariq–*Jebel al-Tariq*) invaded Spain. Beginning in 718, under Pelagius of Asturias, and continuing some 750 years, Spain was reconquered–the *Reconquista*–for Christendom. The last Muslims were expelled in 1492 by Ferdinand and Isabella.
711-750	Conquered the Caucasus.
716-718	Second Arab attack and siege of Constantinople.
718	Aquitaine invaded by Arab forces and attack on Terragone, Italy.
718	Conquest of the Iberian Peninsula (Spain and Portugal) completed. The region was renamed *Al-Andalus*
720	Attacked Narbonne, France.
725	Attacked Carcassonne, France and Muslim occupation of Nimes, France.
730	Attacked Cerdegna, Italy.

732	*Muslim forces attacking Western Europe were finally stopped at Battle of Poitiers near Tours, France. This was regarded as one of the turning points in world history. The Franks, under their leader Charles Martel (the grandfather of Charlemagne), defeated the Muslims and turned them back out of France. The battle determined that Christianity, rather than Islam, would dominate Europe.*
735	Attacked Arles, France.
736	Conquered Tbilisi, Georgia.
750	*In the Middle East, the fall of the Umayyads as the Abbasids established their power.*
751	Arab Muslim forces defeated the Chinese in the Talas River region in present-day Kazakhstan.
756	Umayyads controlled most of Spain and Portugal.
792	Muslim invasion of southern France.
805	Muslim campaigned against the Byzantines; Captured the islands of Rhodes and Cyprus.
813	Attacked Calabria, Italy.
827	Beginning of numerous attacks on Sicily finally conquered in 902 at Taomina.
827-902	Conquered southern Italy.
838	Attacked Marseilles, France.
840	Attacked Tarento, Italy and conquered Crete.
849	Began numerous attacks on Ostia, Italy.
856	Attacked Naples, Italy.
870	Attacked Malta.
878	Attacked Syracuse, Italy.
909	*The Fatimid Caliphate was established in North Africa.*
934	Attacked Genoa, Italy.

969	The Fatimids completed their conquest of Egypt and established a new capital at *al-Qāhirat* (Cairo).
969-1076	*Rule of Syria by the Fatimids.*
c.970	*Seljuk Turks began their invasion of Caliphate lands, taking Baghdad in 1055, and occupied Syria and the Land of Israel (1070-1080).*
1021	*Muslim Druze sect was founded by Caliph al-Hakim.*
1053	The Muslim Almoravids began conquering kingdoms south of the Sahara, including Takrur (in present-day Senegal), Sanhaja, Sijilmasa (1054), and Aoudaghost in 1055.
1062	Muslim Almoravid forces, under Abu Bakr ibn-Umar, attacked the Kingdom of Ghana and by 1076, the Ghanaian capital of Kumbi was captured.
August 26, 1071	Seljuk Turks under Sultan Alp Arslan defeat Byzantines under Emperor Romanus IV at Battle of Manzikert and extended Islam into the Byzantine Empire. The victory allowed the Seljuk Turks to consolidate control of the central Anatolian plateau. They cut off pilgrim routes to Jerusalem, prompting the First Crusade.
1095	*First Crusade was launched to take back the Christian lands.*
1095-1192	*The Crusaders combated Muslims in the Holy Land. It should be understood that the European Crusades of the 10th-13th centuries were not "invasions" by outside powers into the Middle East, but rather an attempt by Christendom to recapture those lands that had been Christian prior to the Muslim invasion.*

1171	*Salah al-Dīn Yusuf ibn Ayyub (better known as Saladin) declared the Fatimid dynasty at an end, and the establishment of the Ayyubid dynasty which ruled Egypt and Syria.*
July 4, 1187	Triggering the Third Crusade, Saladin defeated Guy of Lusignan, King of Jerusalem, at the Battle of Hattin near Tiberias and captured the True Cross. Muslim forces proceeded to conquer Nablus, Jaffa, Ashkelon, Acre, Sidon, Beirut, and Jerusalem (October 2).
January 1189	"I shall cross this sea to their islands to pursue them until there remains no one on the face of the earth who does not acknowledge Allah."– Saladin.
1249	*Under King Afonso III, Portugal became the first Iberian nation liberated from Muslim rule as part of the* Reconquista.
1250-1260	*The Mamluke Sultanate emerged in Egypt and Syria with the decay of the Ayyubid Empire.*
1258	*The Mongols, led by Hulagu Khan, stormed Baghdad, ending the Abbasid caliphate as the Muslim Empire collapsed.*
c. 1290 -1320	Ottoman Turkish states emerged in western Anatolia.
1299-1453	Byzantine Christian-Muslim Ottoman Turkish Wars.
1308	Muslim forces attacked into Thrace, in the Balkans.
1326-1366	Muslim Ottoman Turks conquered western Anatolia, Bursa (1326), Nicaea (1331), Gallipoli (1354), and Adrianople (1366). Continuous attacks began on Thrace, Greece, and Macedonia.

September 26, 1371	Decisive Muslim Turk victory at the Battle of Cirmen; New Muslim incursions into Macedonia and Bulgaria began.
1371-1375	Muslim Ottoman invasion of Serbia.
1388	Northeastern Bulgaria fell to the Muslim Turks.
June 15, 1389	Decisive Muslim defeat of the Serbs and Bosnians at the Field of the Blackbirds, in the Battle of Kosovo. Serbia was placed under *dhimmitude* status.
1421	Renewed attacks were made on the Peloponnesus, Albania, Serbia, and Hungary.
November 10, 1444	The Muslim Turkish forces of Sultan Murad II defeated the Polish and Hungarian armies under Władysław III of Poland and János Hunyadi at the Battle of Varna. By this victory the Turks consolidated their hold on Bulgaria and helped set the stage for the fall of Constantinople.
May 29, 1453	Constantinople fell to Ottoman Turkish forces led by Sultan Mehmed II after a siege. During the battle the Byzantine emperor Constantine XI was killed, thus ending the Byzantine Empire. The Ottomans made the city the capital of the Caliphate and empire. Muslim forces began expansion into Europe from the east.
1456	Muslims conquered Athens, Greece.
1463	Bosnia defeated and annexed by Muslim forces.
1478	Serbia and the Crimea came under Muslim Turkish control.
1480	Otranto in Italy was captured by the Muslims.
1483	Herzegovina defeated and conquered.
1492	*The last Muslims in Granada were defeated and driven out of Spain by Ferdinand and Isabella.*
1512	Muslim forces attacked and defeated Moldavia.
1516-1517	Ottoman Turks conquered Syria and Egypt destroying the Mamluke Sultanate.
August 1521	Captured Belgrade, Serbia.

1522	Turkish Muslim conquest of Rhodes.
1526-1857	Conquered and ruled much of the Indian subcontinent.
August 29, 1526	Suleiman the Magnificent of the Ottoman Empire, defeated and killed the last Jagiellonian king of Hungary and Bohemia at the Battle of Mohács. The Muslim victory threatened Austrian lands.
1527-1543	The Muslim Sultanate of Adal invaded Ethiopia. Muslim forces were led by Ahmed ibn Ibrahim al-Ghazi, the Gragn. Three-quarters of Ethiopia was brought under Muslim control as they sacked churches and monasteries, destroying centuries of literature and art.
1529	First, though unsuccessful, siege of Vienna by the Muslim Ottoman Turks.
1529-1533	Continued attacks in the Danube valley, ended in the Treaty of 1533, when a large portion of eastern Hungary was ceded to the Ottoman Turkish Empire.
1565	*The Muslims were defeated after they besieged Malta.*
1570-1571	Muslim Turks conquered Cyprus.
1571	*Muslims defeated at the naval Battle of Lepanto, led by Don Juan of Austria.*
September 11-12, 1683	*A combined Polish-Austrian-German force led by Jan III Sobieski, the King of Poland, demolished the invading Islamic army of Turks and Tartars at the Battle of Vienna, Austria. The battle was the high-water-mark and turning point in the 300-year struggle between the forces of the Christian Central European kingdoms, and the Turkish/Muslim armies attempting to conquer Europe from the east.*
1696	*Catherine the Great's Russian forces captured Azov giving them access to the Black Sea.*

1696	Muslim Omani forces conquered Mombassa (in present-day Kenya), Pemba, Kilwa, and Zanzibar (all in present-day Tanzania).
August 5, 1716	*Prince Eugene of Savoy defeated the Muslim Turks at Peterwardein after their conquests of Crete and Greece. The resulting Treaty of Passorowitz (1718) caused the Turks to quit Hungary; cede Belgrade and parts of Walachia to Austria; and to surrender portions of Albania and Dalmatia to Venice.*
1774	*A Russian-Turkish War (begun in 1768) ended as Catherine the Great's Russian armies defeated the Turks. This ended a series of attacks on southern Poland and Russia by Muslim forces, and culminated in the Treaty of Kuchuk Kainarji, negotiated and signed July 10-21.*
1783	*Russian forces captured and annexed the Crimea.*
1787	*Muslim Turks were defeated again, ending their influence in southern Poland and Russia.*
1804	Muslim Fulani forces began a jihad that conquered Hausaland (much of present-day northern Nigeria and northern Cameroon).
1817-1837	Muslim Fulani began attacking the Oyo Empire (in present-day western Nigeria) and by 1837 the capital, Old Oyo, was conquered and burned.
1887-1889	Muslim Mahdist forces invaded Ethiopia from Sudan.
March 10, 1889	*The Battle of Metemma (Gallabat). Ethiopian forces commanded by Emperor Yohannes IV, all but defeated the Muslim Mahdist Sudanese army, though Yohannes himself was killed by a sniper's bullet.*

TABLE 11
Recent examples of continued Muslim expansion

DATE	EVENT
June 13, 1915-1923	Muslim Turks massacred approximately 1.5 million Armenians, 750,000 Assyrians, 400,000 Greeks and replaced them with Turks in the west.
1918	*End of Ottoman Turkish rule in Arab areas.*
1921-1922	Muslim Turkey expelled approximately 1,200,000 Greeks from its territory and replaced them with Turks.
1947 to date	The Arab League, now numbering 21 nations, have fought a continual war, both large scale and terrorist, since 1947, in an attempt to destroy the Jewish state of Israel, occupy all its territory, and make the Middle East exclusively Muslim and judenrein ("cleansed of Jews"). 55 of the 57 Islamic nations in the Organization of the Islamic Conference publicly approve of this action.
1947-1976	Muslims expelled approximately 880,000 Jews from their Arab homelands.
1947-to date	There were repeated Muslim attempts, by war and terrorism, to gain control of Kashmir. The Hindus of Pakistan steadily declined, from 15% (in 1947) to 1.5% of the population today.
1947-to date	The Hindus and other non-Muslims fled from Bangladesh (prior to 1971—East Pakistan), where non-Muslims now make up not 35% (in 1947) but 8% of the population.
1949-1967	During the Jordanian occupation of Judea and Samaria (what the Arabs call the "West Bank"), having driven out all the Jews from the area, the Muslim Arabs undertook an unsuccessful attempt to make Jerusalem an exclusively Muslim city by forcing out approximately 14,000 Christian inhabitants.

1955-1972, 1983-to date	Muslim Arab northern Sudan conquered much of southern Sudan, waging genocidal war to convert its Christian and animist population.
1963	Muslim Indonesia occupied all of non-Islamic western New Guinea and incorporated it into Indonesia.
1963-to date	Muslim Malays clashed with the Chinese of Singapore forced the latter's exit from the Federation of Malaysia in 1965. The non-Muslims—Chinese and Hindus—of Malaysia, have seen their relative numbers steadily go down, as the fierce pressure to convert to Islam (not least on the indigenous tribes) has only increased as the new Muslim majority feels the need to exercise its power.
Late 1960s-to date	On-going Muslim insurgency in the southern Philippines, with the goal of a separate Muslim state.
1970-to date	Muslim Northern Nigeria launched religious violence against the largely Christian south.
1974-to date	Muslim Turkey invaded and occupied northern Cyprus, displacing over 200,000 Greek-Cypriots living there
1975-2000	Muslim Indonesia invaded and occupied Christian Timor Este (East Timor). The Indonesian occupation was marked by extreme violence and brutality.
1979	"We shall export our revolution throughout the world … until the calls 'there is no god but Allah and Muhammad is the messenger of Allah' are echoed all over the world."–Ayatollah Ruhollah Khomeini.
1988	The Soviet Union left Afghanistan, defeated by the Muslim mujahadeen. *It was a major victory for Islam over the "West."*

1990s-to date	Muslim Albania is attempting to enlarge its borders at Christian Macedonia's expense.
1994-1996, 1999-to date	Muslims attempted to create an independent Chechnya from Russian territory. This led to two wars and continued terrorist activity.
1998-to date	Muslim Indonesia continued its attempt to destroy Christianity in Sulawesi (formerly the Celebes) and elsewhere in the country. Estimated death toll of over 10,000.
1999-to date	Muslim Kosovo ethnically cleansed its territory of Christian Serbs. Some 200,000-250,000 have already fled.
Sept. 11, 2001	Al-Qaeda attacked the United States, destroying the World Trade Center in New York and damaging the Pentagon, in Washington, D.C. 2,973 were killed.
November 2001	"I was ordered to fight people until they say there is no god but Allah, and his Prophet Muhammad."–Osama bin Laden.
July-Aug. 2006	The Islamic terrorist group, Hezbollah, attacked Israel (Second Lebanon War), which lasted 34 days.

Appendix 13
THE ARAB (JORDANIAN) OCCUPATION OF JERUSALEM

1948-1967

At the end of the first Arab war against the State of Israel—the Israeli War of Independence—Jerusalem was divided, with East Jerusalem and the walled Old City, under Jordanian occupation and cut off from Israeli Jerusalem. Thus the Jordanians controlled 36 out of the 39 holy sites in Jerusalem, sacred to Christianity, Judaism, and Islam.

The Jordanian occupation of Jerusalem was recognized by only one nation, Pakistan. Despite the UN 1949 resolution, which called for all of Jerusalem to be "under a permanent international regime" no action was taken to end the Jordanian occupation.

No Arab state recognized Jordan's subsequent annexation of the Old City in 1950. The April 3, 1949 Israel-Jordan Armistice Agreement (Article VIII), provided for and guaranteed:

". . . free movement of traffic on roads, including the Bethlehem and Latrun-Jerusalem roads; resumption of the normal functioning of the cultural and humanitarian institutions on Mount Scopus and free access thereto; free access to the Holy Places and cultural institutions and use of the cemetery on the Mount of Olives, . . ."

Thus access was assured for Jews to visit the Western Wall (***Hakotel Hamaravi***). But in fact, Jordan denied access to the Old City. Neither Israeli Jews, nor Israeli Christians, nor Israeli Muslims, were allowed access to any of their Holy Places.

The Jordanian Arab Legion illegally expelled the Old City's ancient Jewish community. The world watched unmoved (three years after the Holocaust). It couldn't be bothered (less than a decade after ***Kristallnacht***) when the Jordanians desecrated and destroyed the Jewish Quarter of the Old City.

Jewish academies, libraries, and no fewer than 74 synagogues including the famous Tiferet Yisrael and Rabbi Yehuda Hahasid synagogues, were razed. The ruined remnants of some synagogues were converted into donkey stables, cowsheds, and public lavatories. Hundreds of Torah scrolls and thousands of prayer books were burned. The Tomb of Simon the Just was desecrated and used as a stable. The Western Wall was desecrated by slums and became an outdoor public urinal. On the Mount of Olives, the oldest Jewish cemetery in the world was desecrated as a motor road was built through it, and the Intercontinental Hotel was built atop the mount.

No less than 75% (38,000 of 50,000) of the tombstones in the Mount of Olives Cemetery were ripped out, vandalized, and stolen.

Many ended up in the Jordanian Army camp in Bethany, where they were used as building material in barracks; retaining walls, pathways and latrines. Some were used to construct public urinals near the Western Wall. These actions were not the results of war but deliberate abuse intended to degrade. On Mount Scopus, the Hadassah Hospital and the Hebrew University campus were unused as the Jordanians refused to permit educational and cultural activities on the site, despite a clause in the Armistice agreement, to do so.

Christian pilgrims to the Holy Land, from around the world, who wanted to visit the Holy sites connected with Jesus, e.g. Nazareth, the Sea of Galilee etc., were forced to go to Jordan first, to visit Holy sites and then were permitted by one exit, the Mandlebaum Gate, to enter Israel or what the Arabs/Jordanians called "occupied territory of Palestine." They could not enter from Israel to Jordan. Israeli Christians were only allowed to visit Jerusalem on Christmas day, but only for a few hours.

Appendix 14
Some Historic Occupations

TABLE 12
SOME HISTORIC OCCUPATIONS

AREA	SQ. MILES	OCCUPYING NATION	FROM/TO STATUS
Estonia	17,462	Soviet Union	1940-1991
Latvia	24,938	Sovet Union	1940-1991
Lithuania	25,174	Soviet Union	1940-1991
Gaza Strip	139	Egypt	1948-1967
Judea-Samaria ("West Bank")	2,263	Jordan	1948-1967
Tibet	471,700	China	1950 to date
Sinai Peninsula	23,200	Israel	1967-1982
Abu Musa & the Tunb Islands	9.5	Iran	1971 to date
Aouzou Strip	37,000	Libya	1973-1987
Northern Cyprus	1,295	Turkey	1974 to date
East Timor	5,794	Indonesia	1975-2000
Western Sahara	102,600	Morocco	1976 to date
Lebanon	4,015	Syria	1976-2005
Southern Lebanon	328	Israel *	1985-2000
Gaza Strip	139	Israel **	1967-2005
Judea-Samaria ("West Bank")	2,263	Israel **	1967 to date
Golan Heights	451	Israel ***	1967 to date

* On May 17, 1983, a peace treaty was concluded between Israel and Lebanon. Among the provisions was joint Israeli-Lebanese control of the region to prevent its use by terrorist groups. Massive Syrian pressure forced the Lebanese government to suspend the treaty. When the treaty collapsed, the Israelis elected to control the region on their own with the support of the South Lebanon army.

** In international law, Israel is the successor state to British Mandatory Palestine. It is in dispute/conflict with Palestinian Arabs over possession of this land. Both the Gaza Strip and Judea-Samaria (what the Arabs call "the West Bank") are disputed territory, not a nation or parts of a nation that can be "occupied."

*** The documents establishing the Palestine Mandate (under the League of Nations) signed by Great Britain as the Mandatory, and the League of Nations, became a binding treaty in international law. The resolution of the League of Nations creating the Palestine Mandate included the following significant statement:

> "ART. 5. The Mandatory shall be responsible for seeing that no Palestine territory shall be ceded or leased to, or in any way placed under the control of the Government of any foreign Power."

In 1923, Great Britain transferred the Golan Heights from Mandatory Palestine to the French Mandate of Syria under a Franco-British agreement delineating the boundary between the two mandates. This was in clear violation of Article 5 as outlined above. Thus there is a legal question as to the status of the Golan Heights belonging to Syria. Israel is the legal successor state to Mandatory Palestine.

On June 30, 1939, France detached the Sanjak of Alexandretta from Syria and ceded it to Turkey. To date Syria has never recognized this transfer of territory terming it illegal. The Syrians cannot have it both ways. If they insisted on return of Alexandretta, then Israel had the right and strong legal case to insist on return of the Golan Heights, which is an area in dispute–and not occupied.

While the issue of Israeli "occupation" of Judea-Samaria, Gaza, the Golan Heights, and until 1982, the Sinai Peninsula, was brought up repeatedly at the United Nations and other international forums like the Organization of African Unity (now the African Union), most of the others never were discussed, despite those occupations lasting for longer periods of time and involving larger areas of territory.

Appendix 15
Dhimmi Status

Examples of *dhimmitude*:

- Christians and Jews had to pay a special head tax–*jizya*–mandated in the *Qur'an* as a token of acceptance of the supremacy of Islam. They also had to pay an *avania*, or "protection" payment for their safety and well being as well as the *kharaj*–a tenant tax that acknowledged the land belonged to their Muslim masters.
- Christians and Jews had to bow to their Muslim masters when they paid their taxes (*jizya*). This tax had to be paid in person by each subject, and it had to be paid in a public and humiliating manner.
- Christians and Jews were excluded from holding public office and kept from professions that might make them superior in any way over Muslims.
- Christians and Jews could not give testimony in courts in cases involving Muslims, even if wronged by Muslims. Often Christians and Jews had to hire Muslim "witnesses" to give testimony on their behalf.
- Christians and Jews were often confined to special quarters (e.g. the Christian Quarter and the Jewish Quarter in the

Old City of Jerusalem)–in effect ghettos. In Morocco these ghettos were called *mellahs*. These areas were usually closed after dark. They were not allowed to enter certain streets in Muslim towns and cities.

- Christians and Jews had to get permission to construct buildings. In all cases, the houses of Christians and Jews could never be taller or more elaborate than the houses of their Muslim neighbors.
- Christians and Jews were only allowed to restore any place of worship that needed repair. The construction of new churches and synagogues was forbidden. Christian and Jewish places of worship were often ransacked, burned or demolished at the whim of the Muslims. This practice continues to the present day, witness the desecration of the Church of the Nativity in Bethlehem in 2002, the repeated destruction of the traditional Joseph's Tomb in Shchem (Nablus) in 1996, 2000, and 2003 and the recent desecration of the traditional tomb of the Biblical Joshua at Timnat Haress, near Ariel in Samaria on December 18, 2007.
- Christians and Jews could not pray loudly, ring bells, trumpet shofars (ram's horns used in Jewish ceremonies), or other religious noises within the hearing of any Muslim.
- Christians and Jews had to bury their dead without loud lamentations and prayers. Christian and Jewish graves had to be specially marked to prevent a Muslim from accidentally praying over the grave of an infidel. The cemeteries of Christians and Jews were not respected since they were considered as being from the realm of hell. Commonly they were desecrated or even destroyed completely, as was the

case with the oldest Jewish cemetery on the Mount of Olives in Jerusalem, during the Jordanian occupation, 1949-1967.
- Christians and Jews were prohibited from visibly displaying religious symbols (e.g. crucifixes, icons, or Stars of David).
- Christians could not proselytize on pain of death.
- Christians and Jews were generally prohibited from publishing or sale of non-Muslim religious literature and banned from teaching the *Qur'an*.
- Christians and Jews were prohibited from critique of Muslim holy texts, denial of Muhammad's status as prophet,* and disrespectful references to Islam (recall the controversy over the Danish cartoons in 2005 and the naming of a teddy bear by British school teacher Gillian Gibbons in Sudan in 2007).
- Christian and Jewish communities were religiously harassed and sometimes forced to convert. For example, in Yemen, it was required that every Jewish orphan child be converted to Islam.
- Christians and Jews could not bear arms. In fact, Christians and Jews were not allowed to raise a hand against their Muslim master, even if in self defense. Such an act often resulted in the death penalty.
- Christians and Jews could not ride horses or camels. While they were allowed to ride donkeys, they were required to dismount upon meeting a Muslim and pass him on foot to show their inferior status.
- Christians and Jews had to greet a Muslim first when traveling on a road, and walk in the narrowest part of it. In many countries the Jews were even required to go barefoot. They were also required to walk to the left of the Muslims, discouraging a hostile engagement.

- Christians and Jews could not enter into sexual relations or marriage with Muslim women, upon pain of death. Muslim men, on the other hand, were allowed to marry Christian and Jewish women because the enslavement of non-Muslims by Muslims was allowed.
- Christians and Jews were required to wear distinctive clothing (e.g. *zunar*–wide belts and distinctive conical hats) and colors (e.g. yellow badges). This requirement that they wear a patch of a distinct color on their outer garments was intended to humiliate as well as to allow their recognition as inferior beings.
- In recent times, during negotiations between Arabs and Israelis, the Arabs would not sit in the same room with Israelis to negotiate. For example in 1948-1949, American mediator, Ralph Bunche, had to shuttle between rooms at the same hotel. Henry Kissinger, in 1973-1975, had to shuttle between Jerusalem and Cairo, and Jerusalem and Damascus. The only exceptions were at international forums such as the United Nations General Assembly, the Madrid Middle East Conference of 1991, and the Annapolis Conference of 2007. It should be emphasized however, that at the latter event, the Arabs demanded and the United States acquiesced to having the Israelis enter via a service entrance, thus endorsing the concept of *dhimmitude*.

* It should be noted that Muhammad is regarded, in the Qur'an, as ***uswa hasana***–an "excellent model of conduct" (33.21) and ***al-insan al-kamil***–the universal man; the prototype of all of creation, and the norm of all perfection–i.e. the "perfect man."

Appendix 16
Famous Kings, Queens, and Pharaohs of Egypt

TABLE 13
Famous kings, queens, and pharaohs of Egypt

KING or PHARAOH	YEAR OF REIGN	KEY FACTS
ARCHAIC PERIOD	c. 3100-2770 BCE	Dynasties 1-3
Menes also known as Narmer	3110-2884 BCE	King of Upper Egypt, Menes conquered Lower Egypt and united the two kingdoms. He founded the First dynasty. Capital at Memphis
OLD KINGDOM	2700-2160 BCE	Dynasties 4-7 Worship of kings began. Age of the pyramids.

Khufu or Cheops	2680-2565 BCE	Khufu built the greatest of the Great Pyramids at Giza. The largest pyramid ever built, it was 481' high, 756' long on each side, covering 13 acres, made of 2,300,000 blocks each averaging 2 ½ tons, with the largest weighting 15 tons. According to Herodotus it took 100,000 men twenty years to build it. It was considered one of the Seven Wonders of the Ancient World.
FIRST INTERMEDIATE PERIOD	2200-2050 BCE	Dynasties 9-11
MIDDLE KINGDOM	2134-1786 BCE	Dynasties 12-14
SECOND INTERMEDIATE PERIOD	1786-1560 BCE	Dynasties 15-17
NEW KINGDOM– THE EMPIRE	1575-1087 BCE	Dynasties 18-20 Capital moved to Thebes.
Ahmose I	1580-1557 BCE	Defeated and ousted the Hyksos from Egypt. Founder of the 18th Dynasty and of the New Kingdom. He was first to assume the title pharaoh.

Hatshepsut	1486-1468 BCE	First great woman ruler in history. She increased women's rights in Egypt. Her reign was peaceful. She developed Egypt's resources and expanded foreign trade.
Thutmose III	1468-1436 BCE	Thutmose conquered many lands in southwestern Asia and build a great empire that reached to the Euphrates River. He adopted new techniques of warfare and is considered the "Napoleon of Egypt."
Amenhotep IV or Akhenaton	1375-1358 BCE	Akhenaton introduced monotheism to Egypt. He wanted the Egyptians to worship only one God, the sun-disk god Aton. His wife was the beautiful Queen Nefertiti. He built a new capital: Akhetaten. He may have been murdered.
Tutankhamun III	1361-1352 BCE	King Tut died as a youth. His tomb was discovered in 1922 by British archaeologist Howard Carter. It yielded rich art treasures made of gold, ivory, and precious stones.

Ramses II	1279-1213 BCE	Ramses was probably the pharaoh of the Exodus, when Moses led the Hebrew people out of Egypt. Ramses built a new capital at Tanis (called Ramses) and built many temples and erected large statues of himself.
Ptolemy I	323-284 BCE	Ptolemy founded the great library at Alexandria.
Cleopatra	69-30 BCE	Cleopatra formed an alliance with Julius Caesar of Rome. Caesar helped her win the kingdom from her brother. Later she allied with Marc Antony. She was the last pharaoh of Egypt.

APPENDIX 17
THE LEAGUE OF ARAB STATES

Formed: March 22, 1945. Headquarters: Cairo, Egypt ❖
Charter members: Egypt, Iraq, Jordan (originally Trans-Jordan), Lebanon, Saudi Arabia, Syria, and Yemen ▲

TABLE 14

Additional members of the Arab League

NATION	DATE OF ENTRY	NATION	DATE OF ENTRY
Libya ✦	Mar. 28, 1953	Oman	Sept. 29, 1971
Sudan	Jan. 9, 1956	United Arab Emirates	Dec. 6, 1971
Morocco and Tunisia	Oct. 1, 1958	Mauritania	Nov. 28, 1973
Kuwait	July 20, 1961	Somalia	Feb. 14, 1974
Algeria	Aug. 16, 1962	"Palestine" (PLO)	Sept. 6, 1976
P.D.R. Yemen ▲	Dec. 12, 1967	Djibouti	Sept. 4, 1977
Bahrain and Qatar	Sept. 11, 1971	Comoros	Nov. 20, 1993

Eritrea was given observer status at the Arab League in January 2003.

❖ In March 1979, Egypt was suspended from the Arab League. The headquarters was moved to Tunis, Tunisia. In March 1989, Egypt was re-admitted to the Arab League and the headquarters was returned to Cairo.

▲ May 22, 1990–Yemen and P.D.R. Yemen unified into the Republic of Yemen.

✦ October 25, 2002, Libya withdrew from the Arab League. This would have been effective one year later; however Libya cancelled (January 16, 2003), reaffirmed (April 3, 2003), and again cancelled (May 25, 2003) the decision to withdraw.

APPENDIX 18
JUDEA AND SAMARIA

Judea and Samaria are the historically biblical names for the highland regions of the Land of Israel, with Samaria in the north and Judea to the south. They are the definitive and proper political and geographic names for the region and have been in general use since Clearchus, a disciple of Aristotle. These two areas have no other names. These names were used during the League of Nations Mandate period. They appeared in British government documents, and United Nations documents including the UN Partition Plan of 1947. They appeared in U.S. State Department documents, including a July 18, 1948 map. Even as late as 1961, the **Encyclopaedia Britannica** refers to "Judaea" and "Samaria" in an article on "Palestine" (Vol. 17, p. 118).

Trans-Jordan illegally invaded Judea-Samaria in 1948 and as a result of its aggression occupied that region. It then unilaterally annexed the area on April 4, 1950. That illegal annexaton was recognized by only two nations, the United Kingdom and Pakistan.

The Arab League, their Muslim supporters, anti-Israel elements and misojudaic peoples, deliberately sought to rob the region of its correct political and geographic name. They had to fabricate a brand new name for they could find no other name for the territory. Mislabeling was their technique of disinformation and delegitimization. The "West Bank" was the name concocted by King Abdullah I of Trans-Jordan and his British advisors, allowing the king to annex land outside of his artificially "created" kingdom. He then changed the name of his kingdom twice, first to "The Hashemite Kingdom of the Jordan," but that was quickly rejected since it gave the appearance of a kingdom only along the banks of the Jordan River. The name then was changed again to "The Hashemite Kingdom of Jordan." The term "West Bank" eradicates all Jewish historical connection to the area. It is a sad commentary that many in the West, including the political left, many of Israel's supporters, some Israelis themselves, as well as the naïve and self-delusional who think the name does not matter, have acquiesced to this unilateral change of names and use it in common parlance. But the name does matter. Similarly, the Arabs insist on calling the Persian Gulf, the "Arabian Gulf" and Iran's Khuzistan province, "Arabistan." Why then doesn't much of the world call the Persian Gulf "Arabian?" Is there a double standard at work here?

Besides the political origins of the phrase, one must wonder from a geographical perspective how wide a river bank can be? A river bank may be a few feet or so, but not some 30 miles deep from the river! Just because a new name is invented, does not mean the world should adopt it in common usage. Does an aggressor get rewarded with the additional bonus of a geographic name change designed to eradicate the historic name of a region? In March 1939, Germany renamed the present-day Czech Republic, **Böhmen und Mähren** after seizing that land by aggressive act. During World War II, Germany invaded, occupied, and annexed part of Russia calling it **Ostland**. Do we use those terms today? Do we call Mexico the "South Bank" because it borders on the Rio Grande? Should we rename Serbia, the "West Bank" (of Europe) because it lies to the west of the Danube River and re-designate Poland the "East Bank" due to its location east of the Oder-Neisse Rivers?

Long before most of media capitulated to protests over Danish cartoons and statements by the Pope, the media and many in the world, out of fear and intellectual laziness agreed to obfuscate the truth by surrendering the use of the name Judea-Samaria and adopt the term "West Bank."

The Roman emperor Hadrian in 135 CE, after suppressing the Jewish revolt led by Shimon Bar Kokhba, attempted to eradicate Jewish nationhood, statehood, and any connection to the Land of Israel. He renamed the territory *Palestina*—after the Philistines, the ancient adversaries of the Israelites. Seeking to erase the Jewish connection to Jerusalem the Romans razed the city and named the city built atop the rubble, *Aelia Capitolina*. Nevertheless, as late as the 4th century, the Christian author, Epiphanius, referred to *"Palestina, that is Judea."* Despite this *"Palestina"* is still Israel, *Aelia Capitolina* is still Jerusalem and the "West Bank" is still Judea-Samaria.

Appendix 19
Israel's Insecure Borders
1949-1967
And Soon Again?

- The extreme northern part of the Upper Galilee is 7 miles wide.
- From the foot of the Golan Heights to the Mediterranean Sea is 31 miles.
- From the closest point of northern Samaria (what the Arabs call the "West Bank") to Haifa is 22 miles.
- At its narrow waist, where the majority of population centers lie, Israel is 9 or 11 or 15 miles wide.
- From southern Judea (what the Arabs call the "West Bank") to the Gaza Strip is 21 miles.
- At its widest point in the Negev Desert, Israel is 62 miles across (measuring from the southern end of the Dead Sea to the southern end of the Gaza Strip).
- At its southern tip where the city of Eilat is located, Israel is 6 miles across from the Jordanian border to Egypt.

Appendix 20
The Jewish Connection to Jerusalem

No place on earth touches the soul of the Jewish people as deeply as Jerusalem. The role Jerusalem occupies in Jewish consciousness is unique in the pages of history.

Ancient "Zion" is an actual place–Mount Zion in Jerusalem. It is here that one may find today, the Tomb of King David, the Cenacle–the room of the Last Supper, and Dormition Abbey where tradition states the Virgin Mary fell into an eternal sleep. It was conquered by King David 3,000 years ago and was the site of the two holy Temples. As such it continues to serve as the emotional and spiritual home for the Jewish people.

Since the rule of King David c. 1010-968 BCE, the only nation of which Jerusalem has been the capital is the Jewish nation. It was the capital of the first Jewish kingdom c.1010-586 BCE and the second Jewish kingdom, 520 BCE-70 CE. As such, the Jewish presence in Jerusalem is described in the Bible, reinforced by archaeological evidence, and numerous ancient documents.

Jerusalem became the united capital of the modern State of Israel, by two wars of liberation. Both wars, in 1947-1949 and again in 1967, were launched by the aggression of the Arabs. Israel merely defended itself. In the first, Israel regained control of the western section of the city. It would have gained total control but Jordan's King Abdullah I, listening to his British advisers, agreed to an armistice before he lost it all.

For nineteen years thereafter eastern Jerusalem was under Jordanian occupation and illegally annexed. Jordan violated (with the world silent) those same 1949 armistice agreements, which provided for free access to all the Jewish religious sites in the Old City, including the Western Wall, and beyond, including the Mount of Olives Cemetery. The Old Jewish Quarter of the city was totally desecrated and destroyed.

In June 1967, despite Israeli appeals, via three different message-routes, the Jordanians attacked and lost control of the eastern portion of the city that they illegally occupied in 1949. Thus the eastern portion of the city was liberated in June 1967 only after Jordan attacked Israel. It was then proclaimed on two occasions the united capital of Israel.

While it served as a capital of the Crusader "Kingdom of Jerusalem" for 88 years, the Crusaders were not a nation. It has never served as an Arab capital for the simple reason that there has never been a Palestinian Arab state.

The Jews are the only people who have inhabited Jerusalem continuously–with relatively short interruptions imposed by bans of conquerors–for 3,000 years. From the early 19th century Jews constituted the largest ethnic group in the city, and by the end of the 19th century they had become an absolute majority—a position they have kept for over 100 years.

There is no equivalent in any culture for Jewish prayers, some of them going all the way back to biblical times. *Psalm 137* admonishes the Jewish people: "If I forget thee, O Jerusalem, let my right hand forget her cunning. If I do not remember thee, let my tongue cleave to the roof of my mouth; if I prefer not Jerusalem above my highest joy." The city is mentioned 657 times in the Hebrew Bible and 154 times in the New Testament. It should be noted that the **Qur'an** never mentions Jerusalem–not even once.

No matter where Jews lived throughout the world, as the Diaspora, for 1,875 years, their thoughts and prayers were directed toward Jerusalem. Despite centuries of exile, the Jews maintained a continuous presence in Jerusalem. Even today, whether in Israel, the United States or anywhere else, Jewish ritual practice, holiday celebration, and lifecycle events include recognition of Jerusalem as a core element of the Jewish experience. Consider that:

- Jews in prayer always turn toward Jerusalem.
- Arks (the sacred chests) that hold Torah scrolls in synagogues throughout the world face Jerusalem.
- Jews end Passover Seders each year with the words: "Next year in Jerusalem;" the same words are pronounced at the end of Yom Kippur, the most solemn day of the Jewish year.
- A three-week moratorium on weddings in the summer recalls the breaching of the walls of Jerusalem by the Chaldean (New Babylonian) army in 586 BCE. That period culminates

in a special day of mourning—Tisha B'Av (the 9th day of the Hebrew month Av)—commemorating the destruction of both the First and Second Temples.
- Jewish wedding ceremonies—joyous occasions, are marked by sorrow over the loss of Jerusalem. The groom recites a biblical verse from the Babylonian Exile: "If I forget thee, O Jerusalem, let my right hand forget her cunning," and breaks a glass in commemoration of the destruction of the Temples.

Even body language, often said to tell volumes about a person, reflects the importance of Jerusalem to Jews as a people and, arguably, the lower priority the city holds for Muslims:

- When Jews pray they face Jerusalem; in Jerusalem Israelis pray facing the Temple Mount.
- When Muslims pray, they face Mecca; in Jerusalem Muslims pray with their backs to the city.
- Even at burial, a Muslim face is turned toward Mecca.

David Ben-Gurion, who would become Israel's first Prime Minister, had as a rule infused major public addresses with historical references to the Land of Israel and to Jerusalem. In a speech to the 21st Zionist Congress, in Basel, Switzerland, in 1937 he stated:

"No Jew is at liberty to surrender the right of the Jewish Nation and the Land of Israel to exist. No Jewish body is sanctioned to do so. No Jew alive today has the authority to yield any piece of land whatsoever. This right is preserved by the Jewish people throughout the generations and cannot be forfeited under any circumstance. Even if at some given time there will be those who declare that they are relinquishing this right, they have neither the power nor the jurisdiction to negate it for future generations to come. The Jewish Nation is neither obligated by nor responsible for any waiver such as this. Our right to this land, in its entirety, is steadfast inalienable and eternal. And until the coming of the Great Redemption, we shall never yield this historic right."

Ben-Gurion, reminded the Israeli Parliament, the Knesset, in 1949: "Our ties today with Jerusalem are no less deep than those which existed in the days of Nebuchadnezzar and Titus Flavius... our fighting youth knew how to sacrifice itself for our holy capital no less than did our forefathers in the days of the First and Second Temples."

In 1950, Abba Eban, Israel's Foreign Minister, would emphasize this theme at the UN Trusteeship Council: "A devotion to the Holy City has been a constant theme of our people for three thousand years."

At the 1991 Madrid Peace Conference, Prime Minister Yitzhak Shamir told the opening session attended by nearly all the region's Arab leaders, "We are the only people who have lived in the Land of Israel without interruption for nearly 4,000 years; we are the only people, except for a short Crusader kingdom, who have had an independent sovereignty in this land; we are the only people for whom Jerusalem has been a capital; we are the only people whose sacred places are only in the Land of Israel."

Since June 1967, Israel has a proven track record of ensuring full access to the city's holy sites. It allowed all peoples, including citizens of enemy states, e.g. Kuwaiti Muslims, to visit the holy sites.

Appendix 21
The Constantinople Convention on Free Navigation of the Suez Canal

On October 29, 1888, Austria-Hungary, Great Britain, France, Germany, Italy, The Netherlands, Russia, Spain, and Turkey signed the Convention respecting the Free Navigation of the Suez Maritime Canal.

The fundamental provisions of the Convention are contained in Articles 1 and 4 as follows:

"The Suez Maritime Canal shall always be free and open; in time of war as in time of peace, to every vessel of commerce or of war, without distinction of flag . . . The Canal shall never be subjected to the exercise of the right of blockade. Consequently, the high Contracting Parties agree not in any way to interfere with the free use of the canal, in time of war as in time of peace."

"The Maritime Canal remaining open in time of war as a free passage, even to the ships of war of belligerents… the High Contracting Parties agree that no right of war, no act of hostility, nor any act having for its object to obstruct the free navigation of the Canal, shall be committed in the Canal and its ports of access… though the Ottoman Empire should be one of the belligerent Powers." (In terms of the Convention the legal successor to the Ottoman Empire is Egypt.)

The Convention also confirmed and completed the system of international operation embodied by the Universal Suez Canal Company, set up in 1863.

Egypt nationalized the Suez Canal Company in July 1956 (See Appendix 22–Egyptian President Gamal Abdel Nasser nationalizes the Suez Canal, July 26, 1956), an act which was regarded by many users of the Canal as a contravention of the 1888 Convention.

In April 1957, when the Canal was re-opened to navigation, after it had been obstructed for several months, the Egyptian Government issued a declaration in which it stated its intention to respect "the terms and spirit of the Constantinople Convention and the rights and obligations arising therefrom." Despite this pledge it continued to block Israeli flag vessels and cargoes bound to or from Israel on third flag vessels until the Egyptian-Israeli Peace Treaty of 1979.

Appendix 22
Egyptian President Gamal Abdel Nasser Nationalizes the Suez Canal, July 26, 1956

(Annotated)

BACKGROUND

On October 19, 1954, the United Kingdom and Egypt concluded a treaty by which the British would remove its armed forces from the Suez Canal Zone within the next 20 months. An additional provision allowed the British to militarily reoccupy the Zone for the next seven years if Turkey or any Arab country were attacked. Egypt could now use the Suez Canal as a bargaining chip to obtain foreign aid for the construction of the Aswan High Dam. With this knowledge in mind too, Egyptian leader Gamal Abdel Nasser prepared plans for the nationalization of the canal.

On June 12, 1956 the last British troops evacuated the Suez Canal Zone. There was now no roadblock to an Egyptian nationalization of the canal at any time of Nasser's choosing. With the withdrawal of their aid offer to finance the construction of the Aswan High Dam, on July 19, 1956, the United States and the United Kingdom provided Nasser with the pretext needed to proceed.

As the fates would have it, Egypt's seizure of the canal was obscured by a major maritime crisis, as a collision at sea between the *Andrea Doria* and the *Stockholm*, riveted the attention of much of the world, but did not deter Nasser from moving swiftly to seize the canal. His speech, below, was the signal for the canal's takeover.

"This, O citizens, is the battle in which we are now involved. It is a battle against imperialism and the methods and tactics of imperialism, and a battle against Israel, the vanguard of imperialism . . . As I told you; Arab nationalism has been set on fire from the Atlantic Ocean to the Persian Gulf. Arab nationalism feels its existence, its structure and strength . . . . On 18 June we were able to raise in the sky of Egypt the flag of Egypt alone

. . . . Not everyone will sell his country for money [Nasser's criticism of political conditions attached to Western aid] . . . . Do we want arms to dictate our policy or our policy to dictate arms? I do not know whether they are 'Communist arms', or 'non-Communist arms.' In Egypt these arms are Egyptian arms. [Nasser thus admitted that he had received Soviet-supplied arms]"

Characterizing the High Dam negotiations as "long and bitter," Nasser said the West's terms constituted "Imperialism without soldiers." "They are punishing Egypt because she refused to side with military blocs . . . ." "I began to look at Mr. Black [head of the World Bank] sitting in his chair and I imagined that I was sitting in front of Ferdinand de Lesseps. [The name "Ferdinand de Lesseps" was the secret signal for Egyptian forces to seize the canal. It was repeated 14 times in the space of 10 minutes!]"

"One hundred twenty thousand workers died digging the Canal gratis. We dug the canal with our lives, our skulls, our bones, our blood . . . . Instead of the Canal being dug for Egypt, Egypt became the property of the Canal . . . . The Suez Canal Company became a state within a state, one which humiliated ministers . . . It is no shame, for one to be poor and to borrow in order to build up one's country; What is a shame is to suck the blood of, a people and usurp their rights.

The income of the Suez Canal Company in 1955 reached 35 million Egyptian pounds, or 100 million dollars . . . . Do you know how much assistance America and Britain were going to offer us over 5 years? 70 million dollars. Do you know who takes the 100 million dollars the company's income, every year? They take them of course . . . . We shall never repeat the past but we shall eliminate the past by regaining our rights in the Suez Canal. This money is ours and this canal belongs to Egypt because it is an Egyptian limited liability company.

Does history repeat itself? On the contrary! . . . We shall build the High Dam and we shall gain our usurped rights. We shall build the High Dam as we want it . . . The canal company annually takes 35 million Egyptian pounds. Why shouldn't we take it ourselves?

. . . Therefore I have signed today and the government has approved . . . a resolution . . . for the nationalization of the Universal Company of the Suez Maritime Canal.

Today, O citizens, . . . we shall not look for the $70 million of American aid. And whenever any talk comes from Washington I shall tell them: 'Drop dead of our fury.' We shall set up industries and compete with them. They do not want us to become an industrial country so they can promote the sale of their products and market them in Egypt. I never saw any American aid directed toward industrialization . . . . American aid is everywhere directed towards exploitation . . . . In the same way as Farouk left on 26 July 1952, the old Suez Canal Company also saves us on the same day."

Egypt also seized the account of the *Compagnie Universelle du Canal de Suez* (Suez Canal Company) in the Ottoman Bank in Cairo, amounting to E£ 5 million. The British government held 44% of the shares in the company. France also held shares in the company.

The nationalization of the Suez Canal symbolized the modern Arab world's declaration of independence. Nasser correctly calculated that the British had to intervene immediately, if at all, remarking "It must appear as a direct reaction. If [British Prime Minister Anthony] Eden delays, the pressure against him will increase."

Nasser considered that the peak period of danger for Egypt would be 80% at the beginning of August 1956, one week after the nationalization, "decreasing each week through political activities." By the end of September, the danger of British military intervention would be reduced to 20%. Since Nasser estimated that the British could not intervene for at least two months, the chance for Egyptian success in keeping the canal was, to say the least encouraging.

The British and French did intervene militarily, but their intervention only began on October 31st and was stopped before they could achieve their objectives. This case is a classic example of an opponent, which does possess the potential to retaliate against a fair accompli being unable to do so, since he requires an excessive length of time for his military preparations. Similar circumstances befell the United States as the time of the November 1979 seizure of U.S. diplomatic hostages and its embassy in Tehran, Iran.

Appendix 23
UN "Zionism is Racism" Resolution

On November 10, 1975, the United Nations General Assembly (where the United States has no veto) passed a resolution (UNGA 3379) condemning and labeling "Zionism as a form of racism." Before the vote, a ballot to defer the resolution lost by only 12 votes, 67-55.

The final vote for the resolution was:

- 72 in favor (including the Arab and other Islamic nations, almost all African and Asian states, the Soviet Union, and the communist bloc. But also voting for the resolution was:
- India, led by Indira Gandhi, who had destroyed democracy in her own nation and who had been turned into an Arab-Soviet proxy.
- Brazil, seeking Arab oil and investments.
- Mexico, which voted for deferral but then voted for the resolution.
- Iran (of the Shah), Turkey, and Cyprus all of which voted against deferral motion and for the anti-Zionism resolution.
- 35 against (including the U.S., most of Western Europe, Australia, New Zealand, and Israel).

- 32 abstentions including:
- Japan, which voted for deferral, but which abstained on the resolution vote.
- Jamaica and Greece, both of which abstained on both votes and thus helped defeat the deferral motion.

Given that racism had already been defined by the UN as a crime, and given, too, that Zionism was Israel's very **raison d'etre**, this resolution in effect convicted Israel of being an outlaw state. It thereby made a mighty contribution to the campaign on the diplomatic front of the Arab world's war against Israel.

The main objective of this campaign (spearheaded and masterminded in those days by the Soviet Union) was not to force Israel into changing this or that policy or withdrawing from this or that piece of land. It was, rather, to stigmatize the Jewish state as illegitimate in its very essence. Being illegitimate, it had no right to defend itself against attack and if it did so, it was guilty of the added crime of aggression. As the then President of Egypt, Gamal Abdel Nasser, had put it shortly before the outbreak of the Six-Day War of 1967: "Israel's existence is in itself an aggression." Conversely, anyone who might launch an actual aggression of any kind against Israel, whether in the form of terrorist bombings or assault by regular military forces, was, in the topsy-turvy conceptions of the UN, acting in self-defense and in accordance with international law.

Israel's UN Ambassador Chaim Herzog noted the significance of the date:

"This night, 37 years ago, has gone down in history as the **Kristallnacht,** or the Night of the Crystals. This was the night of 10 November 1938 when Hitler's Nazi Storm troopers launched a coordinated attack on the Jewish community in Germany, burnt the synagogues in all the cities and made bonfires in the streets, of the Holy Books and the Scrolls of the Holy Laws and the Bible. It was the night when Jewish homes were attacked and heads of families were taken away, many of them never to return. It was the night when the windows of all Jewish businesses and stores were smashed, covering the streets in the cities of Germany with a film of broken glass which dissolved into millions of crystals, giving that night the name of **Kristallnacht,** the Night of the Crystals."

The United States Ambassador to the United Nations, Daniel Patrick Moynihan, denounced the resolution in an eloquent and widely noticed speech that began and ended with a defiant sentence provided him by Norman Podhoretz of **Commentary** magazine: "The United States rises to declare before the General Assembly of the UN, and before the world, that it does not acknowledge, it will never abide by, it will never acquiesce in this infamous act."

The UN re-adopted that resolution every year for sixteen years. It took sixteen years for the resolution to be revoked.

Anti-Israel and misojudaic invective continued unabated at the UN. Typifying the many statements made and resolutions passed was the 1984 statement by the Saudi Arabian delegate as he spoke before the UN Human Rights Commission Conference on Religious Tolerance: "The Talmud says that if a Jew does not drink every year the blood of a non-Jewish man, he will be damned for eternity."

Ironically, it is this Human Rights Commission which is the most virulent center of anti-Israel activities in the United Nations. It has classified Israel as the principal human rights violator in the whole world; since its inception, about 25% of its resolutions have condemned Israel.

REPEAL OF THE UN "ZIONISM IS RACISM" RESOLUTION

On December 16, 1991, the UN General Assembly Resolution 46/86 simply declared: "The General Assembly Decides to revoke the determination contained in its resolution 3379 (XXX) of 10 November 1975."

The vote was:

- 111 in favor–including the United States, Canada, Europe including the Soviet Union, Latin America and the Caribbean nations, many sub-Saharan African nations, many non-Muslim Asian nations including India, Japan, South Korea, Singapore, and Thailand; Australia, New Zealand, the Pacific nations and Israel.
- 25 against–including Arab and Muslim states of Africa and Asia; Cuba, North Korea, Sri Lanka, and Viet Nam.
- 13 abstain–including Angola, Burkina Faso, Ethiopia, Ghana, Laos, Maldives, Mauritius, Myanmar, Tanzania, Trinidad and Tobago, Turkey, Uganda, and Zimbabwe.

- 15 did not vote–including Bahrain, Chad, China, Comoros, Djibouti, Egypt, Guinea, Guinea-Bissau, Kuwait, Morocco, Niger, Oman, Senegal, Tunisia, and Vanuatu.

It has been the only anti-Israel resolution revoked to date.

On November 10, 2005, the 30th anniversary of the "Zionism is racism resolution," U.S. Ambassador to the UN, John Bolton called the resolution the UN's "single worst decision." He added: "It's incredible that it was passed to begin with" and "It's incredible that it took 16 years to repeal it."

Appendix 24
UN General Assembly Resolution 181– Partition of Palestine

November 29, 1947
(Annotated)

BACKGROUND

While the Arabs in 1947 were a majority of the population in all of Mandatory Palestine (some 1,200,000), the Jews were a majority in the area allotted to them. They numbered 650,000. The Jewish state was already in existence, in all but name.

TABLE 15
UN Partition of Palestine 1947
Land and people

	JEWISH STATE	ARAB STATE
Per cent of land	56	43
Per cent of population	58	99
Groups left in other state	497,000 Arabs	10,000 Jews

1% of the land was to be a *Corpus Separatum* i.e. Jerusalem.

The proposed Jewish state was in the "wrong" parts of the Palestine Mandate, i.e. not in the Biblical Land of Israel e.g. Hebron.

UN General Assembly Resolution 181 delineated a two state solution for Jews and Arabs west of the Jordan River. Both states were to be joined by an economic union and share joint currency. The resolution declared that Arabs and Jews would become "citizens of the State in which they are resident and enjoy full civil and political rights" and that Arabs living in the Jewish state could opt, within one year from the date of the resolution's implementation, for citizenship of the Arab state, and Jews living in the Arab state could opt for citizenship of the Jewish state.

Demilitarized Jerusalem under the UN

The City of Jerusalem was to be demilitarized and placed under a special international regime–a *Corpus Separatum*– to be administered by the United Nations through the Trusteeship Council. But this regime was to be limited in time. It was not to be an "international city" for all time as some have claimed.

"The Statute elaborated by the Trusteeship Council the aforementioned principles shall come into force not later than 1 October 1948. It shall remain in force in the first instance for a period of ten years, unless the Trusteeship Council finds it necessary to undertake a re-examination of these provisions at an earlier date. After the expiration of this period the whole scheme shall be subject to examination by the Trusteeship Council in the light of experience acquired with its functioning. The residents of the City shall be then free to express by means of a referendum their wishes as to possible modifications of regime of the City."

This provision for a referendum was of critical importance to the acceptance of UNGA Resolution 181 by Ben Gurion. He knew that the Jews were in a majority within these boundaries and would be in 10 years when the referendum was to be held. Thus he was confident that Jerusalem would return to Jewish hands.

The Jewish State was to receive the eastern Galilee from the Hulah Basin and the Sea of Galilee in the northeast to the crest of the Gilboa Mountains in the south. The Jewish section of the coastal plain "extends from a point between Minat El-Qila and Nabi Yunis in the Gaza Sub-District and includes the towns of Haifa and Tel Aviv, leaving Jaffa as an enclave of the Arab State." The Jews were also to receive the Negev area, but without the city of Beersheba, and a strip of land along the Dead Sea.

Whereas the Jews were ready to accept a compromise and agree to partition, the Arabs rejected it totally and immediately escalated warfare as soon as the Resolution passed by a vote of 33-13 with 10 abstentions.

Among those voting in favor were the United States, despite a proposal to give the Negev to the Arabs, the Soviet Union, and many Western European and Latin American nations. Of particular note is that Belgium resisted British pressure to vote against or abstain; Costa Rica voted "in favor" despite an Arab attempt to bribe that nation with an offer of support for a high UN position for a Costa Rican delegate.

Voting against as expected were the six Arab members of the UN–Egypt, Iraq, Lebanon, Saudi Arabia, Syria, and Yemen. They were joined by the Muslim nations of Afghanistan, Iran, Pakistan, and Turkey. Additionally India, with a very large Muslim minority voted against, as did Cuba, and Greece, the latter out of fear of Egyptian retaliation on the 150,000 Greeks in Egypt.

The United Kingdom abstained as did Argentina, Chile, China, Colombia, El Salvador, Ethiopia, Honduras, Mexico, and Yugoslavia. The delegate of Thailand (who would have voted "against") was absent, as he was recalled due to a military coup in that country.

SIGNIFICANCE

As a General Assembly resolution, UNGA 181 had no force of international law. The international legal basis for the Jewish state was the 1922 League of Nations Mandate for Palestine which charged the British government with administering the area earmarked as the future Jewish state.

Indeed, if anything, resolution 181 sought to legitimize illegal moves taken by Britain throughout the term of its mandate. As the League of Nations mandate made clear, Britain was supposed to preside over the territory of the Mandatory Palestine and to foster the establishment of a Jewish state which would eventually replace the British mandatory government. UNGA Resolution 181 simply accepted an already existing national entity.

The partition plan merely expressed the willingness of two-thirds of the UN General Assembly to accept the establishment of a Jewish state and an Arab state in Palestine. It did not ensure the establishment of either. There was no enforcement mechanism in place to insure that the General Assembly recommendation be carried out. Indeed even as the Arab countries attacked the new declared Jewish state of Israel, there were no UN moves to halt the aggression, and to declare the Arabs the aggressors. Israel was left to fend for itself in a life or death struggle.

The Jewish state came into existence because the foundations for it had been laboriously laid for several decades. In fact, by 1939, the embryo of a state was already in being–and because the Jewish people were ready to fight for it.

The Arab Palestinian state failed to emerge because no foundations had been laid for it, and its potential citizens did nothing to further its emergence.

Appendix 25
UNITED NATIONS SECURITY COUNCIL RESOLUTION 242 AND 338

The Security Council, Expressing its continuing concern with the grave situation in the Middle East, Emphasizing the inadmissibility of the acquisition of territory by war and the need to work for a just and lasting peace in which every State in the area can live in security;

Emphasizing further that all member States in their acceptance of the Charter of the United Nations have undertaken a commitment to act in accordance with Article 2 of the Charter;

1. Affirms that the fulfillment of Charter principles requires the establishment of just and lasting peace in the Middle East which should include the application of both following principles:

   i) Withdrawal of Israeli armed forces from territories occupied in the recent conflict;
   ii) Termination of all claims or states of belligerency and respect for and acknowledgement of the sovereignty, territorial

integrity and political independence of every State in the area and their right to live in peace within secure and recognized boundaries free from threats or acts of force;

2. Affirms further the necessity:

   a) For guaranteeing freedom of navigation through international waterways in the area;
   b) For achieving a just settlement of the refugee problem;
   c) For guaranteeing the territorial inviolability and political independence of every State in the area, through measures including the establishment of demilitarized zones;

3. Requests the Secretary General to designate a Special Representative, to proceed to the Middle East to establish and maintain contacts with the States concerned in order to promote agreement and assist efforts to achieve a peaceful and accepted settlement in accordance with the provisions and principles in this resolution;

4. Requests the Secretary General to report to the Security Council on the progress of the efforts of the Special Representative as soon as possible.

UNITED NATIONS SECURITY COUNCIL RESOLUTION 338

The Security Council,

1. Calls upon all parties to the present fighting to cease all firing and terminate all military activity immediately, no later than 12 hours after the moment of the adoption of this decision, in the positions they now occupy;

2. Calls upon the parties concerned to start immediately after the cease-fire the implementation of Security Council Resolution 242 (1967) in all of its parts;

3. Decides that immediately and concurrently with the cease-fire, negotiations shall start between the parties concerned under appropriate auspices aimed at establishing a just and durable peace in the Middle East.

Edward N. Luttwak, military analyst, noted in an essay that appeared in 1999, in *Foreign Affairs*: "Cease-fires and armistices have frequently been imposed under the aegis of the Security Council in order to halt fighting. . . . But a cease-fire tends to arrest war-induced exhaustion and lets belligerents . . . rearm their forces. It intensifies and prolongs the struggle once the cease-fire ends–and it does usually end." This has proven to be the case at the imposed end of the 1948-1949 Arab-Israel War, the 1956 Sinai-Suez War, the 1967 Six Day War, the 1967-1970 1000 Day War of Attrition, and the 2006 Second Lebanon War.

Appendix 26
Jewish Population in Arab Countries

TABLE 16

Jewish population in Arab countries

COUNTRY	1948	1976	2001	2008
Morocco	265,000	17,000	5,230	<7,000
Algeria	140,000	500	0	0
Tunisia	105,000	2,000	<1,000	<1,500 (2004)
Libya	38,000	20	0	0
Egypt	100,000	200	100	<100
Iraq	135,000	400	200	<100
Bahrain	550-600	N.A.	36	30
Syria	30,000	4,350	<100	<30
Lebanon	5,000	150	<100	40
Yemen	55,000	1,000	<100	<200
Aden (later South Yemen)	8,000	0	0	0
TOTAL	881,600	25,620	<6,866	<9,000

Suggested Reading

This bibliography is a list of books important to an understanding of Middle East history, politics, and diplomacy. They contain facts and opinions of authors with different perspectives. This bibliography is not annotated so as not to bias the reader in favor or against any given book. This list is not all inclusive. Inclusion of any book should not be construed as endorsement of its opinions and content. This list, however, substantiates the information represented in this book. Most are in the library of the author. Many of these works have several editions. Check Amazon.com, Barnes & Noble.com or similar source for the latest available editions.

GENERAL OVERVIEWS OF THE MIDDLE EAST

Armajani, Yahya and Ricks, Thomas. *Middle East Past and Present,* Second Edition, Prentice-Hall, Englewood, N.J. 1986.

Cleveland, William. *A History of the Modern Middle East,* Second Edition, Boulder, CO., 2000.

Congressional Quarterly. *The Middle East,* Ninth Edition, CQ Press, Washington, D.C., 2000.

Fisher, Sydney N., and Ochsenwald, William. *The Middle East: A History* (in two volumes), 5th edition, McGraw Hill, New York, 1997.

Gale, General Sir Richard. *Great Battles of Biblical History,* John Day, New York, 1970.

Gervasi, Frank. *Thunder over the Mediterranean,* David McKay, New York, 1975.

Herzog, Chaim and Gichon, Mordechai. *Battles of the Bible,* Random House, New York 1978.

Kort, Michael G. *The Handbook of the Middle East,* Twenty-First Century Books, Brookfield, CT, 2002.

Lenczowski, George. *The Middle East in World Affairs,* Fourth Edition, Cornell University Press, Ithaca, N.Y., 1980.

Lewis, Bernard. *A Middle East Mosaic: Fragments of Life, Letters and History,* Random House 2000.

Lewis, Bernard. *The Middle East: A Brief History of the Last 2,000 Years,* Scribners, New York, 1995.

Lewis, Bernard. *The Multiple Identities in the Middle East,* Schoken Books, New York, 1998.

Long, David and Reich, Bernard (Eds.). *The Government and Politics of the Middle East and North Africa,* Westview Press, Boulder, CO, 1986.

Mansfield, Peter. *The Middle East: A Political and Economic Survey,* Oxford University Press, London, 1973.

Ovendale, Ritchie. *The Middle East since 1914*, Second Edition, Longman, London, 1998.

Shimoni, Yaacov. *Biographical Dictionary of the Middle East*, Facts on File, New York, 1991.

Yapp. M.E. *The Near East since the First World War: A History to 1995*, Longman, London, 1996.

ISLAM

Adas, Michael (Ed). *Islamic and European Expansion: The Forging of a Global Order*, Temple University Press, Philadelphia, 1993.

Ali, Abdella Yusuf. Translator, *The Qur'an*, Tahrike Tarsile Qur'an, 1995.

Ankerberg John & Weldon John. *Fast Facts on Islam: What You Need To Know Now*, Harvest House, Eugene, 2001.

Arberry, J. Translator, *The Koran Interpreted*, Touchstone, New York, 1955.

Asad, Muhammad. *The Message of The Qur'an*, (Bilingual edition) The Book Foundation, 2003.

Ben-Shemesh, A. (Translator) *The Noble Qur'an*, Massada Publishing, Tel Aviv, 1979.

Bevan, Edwyn R. & Singer, Charles. (Eds.), *The Legacy of Islam*, Oxford Univ. Press, 1927.

Bostom, Andrew G. *The Legacy of Jihad*, Prometheus, Amherst, 2005.

Bostom, Andrew G. *The Legacy of Islamic Anti-Semitism*, Prometheus, Amherst, 2007.

Caner, Ergun Mehmet. & Caner, Emir Fethi, *Unveiling Islam: An Insider's look at Muslim Life and Beliefs*, Kregel Publications, Grand Rapids, MI, 2002.

Dawood, N.J. Translator, *The Koran*, Penguin, 1999.

Darwish, Nonie. *Now They Call Me Infidel*, Sentinel Books, New York 2006.

Davis, Gregory, M. *Religion of Peace?* World Ahead, Los Angeles, 2006.

Dawood, N.J. *The Koran*, Penguin Classics.

Esposito, John L. (Ed). *The Oxford Encyclopedia of the Modern Islamic World*, Oxford University Press, New York, 2001.

Fregosi, Paul. *Jihad in the West: Muslim Conquests from the 7th to the 21st Centuries*, Prometheus Book, Amherst, NY, 1998.

Goldziher, Igantz. *Introduction to Islamic Theology and Law*, Princeton University Press 1981.

Guillaume, Alfred. *The Traditions of Islam: An Introduction to the Study of the Hadidth Literature*, Khayats, Beirut, 1966.

Guillaume, Alfred. *Islam*, Penguin Books, New York, 1978.

Holt, Peter Malcom and Lambton, Ann K.S. editors. *The Cambridge History of Islam* (2 vols.). 1970, revised 4 vols. 1978.

Harrison, Lawrence & Huntington, Samuel. (Eds..), *Culture Matters: How Values Shape Human Progress*, Basic Books, 2000.

Humphreys, R. Stephen. *Islamic History: A framework for Inquiry*, Princeton Univ. Press 1991.

Karsh, Efraim. *Islamic Imperialism: A History*, Yale University Press, New London, 2007.

Lewis, Bernard. *Islam and the West*, Oxford Univ. Press, 1993.

Lewis, Bernard. *Islam in History: Ideas, People, and Events in the Middle East*, Open Court, Chicago, 1993.

Lewis, Bernard. *The Crisis of Islam: Holy War and Unholy Terror*, Modern Library, New York, 2003.

Lewis, Bernard. *The Muslims Discovery of Europe*, W. W. Norton & Company, New York, 2001.

Manji, Irshad. *The trouble with Islam*, St, Martin Press, New York, 2003.

Meddeb, Abdelwahab. *The Malady of Islam*, Basic Books, New York, 2003.

Margoliouth, G. and Rodwell, J.M., *The Koran*, Dover Publications, 2005.

Nagel, Tilman. *The History of Islamic Theology from Muhammad to the Present*, Marcus Wiener Publishers, Princeton, 2000.

Peters, F.E. *Muhammad and the Origins of Islam*, SUNY Press, Albany, 1994.

Pickthall, M. M. *The Meaning of the Glorious Koran*, Plume, 1997.

Pipes, Daniel. *In the Path of God: Islam and Political Power*, Transactions Publishers, New Brunswick, 2002.

Pipes, Daniel. *Miniatures: Views of Islamic and Middle Eastern Politics*, Transactions Publishers, New Brunswick, 2004.

Rippin, Andrew. *Muslims: Their Religious Beliefs and Practices, Volume 1: The Formative Period*, Routledge, London, 1990.

Roy, Oliver. *The Failure of Political Islam*, Harvard Univ. Press 1996.

Segal, Ronald. *Islam's Black Slaves: The Other Black Diaspora*, Farrar, Straus and Giroux, 2006.

Shorrosh, Anis A. *Islam Revealed: A Christian Arab's View of Islam*, Thomas Nelson Publishers, Nashville, 1988.

Spencer, Robert. *Islam Unveiled: Disturbing Questions about the World's Fastest-growing Faith*, Encounter Books, San Francisco, 2002.

Spencer, Robert. *The Politically Incorrect Guide to Islam (and The Crusades)*, Regnery, 2005.

Spencer, Robert. *The Myth of Islamic Tolerance*, Prometheus, Amherst, 2005.

Spencer, Robert. *The Truth About Muhammad: Founder of the World's Most Intolerant Religion*, Regnery, 2006.

Spencer, Robert and Chesler, Phyllis. *The Violent Oppression of Women in Islam,* David Horowitz Freedom Center, Los Angeles, California, 2007.

Trifkovic, Serge. *The Sword of the Prophet: Islam, History, Theology impact on the World,* Regina Orthodox Press, Boston, 2002.

Warraq, Ibn. *Why I Am Not a Muslim,* Prometheus, Amherst, 1995.

Warraq, Ibn. (Ed), *The Origins of the Koran: Classic Essays on Islam's Holy Book,* Prometheus, Amherst, 1998.

Warraq, Ibn. (Ed), *The Quest for the Historical Muhammad,* Prometheus, Amherst, 2000.

Warraq, Ibn. (Ed), *What the Koran Really Says: Language, Text & Commentary,* Prometheus, Amherst, 2002.

Warraq, Ibn. (Ed), *Leaving Islam: Apostates Speak Out,* Prometheus, Amherst, 2003.

Ye'or, Bat. *Eurabia: The Euro-Arab Axis,* Fairleigh Dickinson University Press, 2005.

Ye'or, Bat. *Islam and Dhimmitude: Where Civilizations Collide,* Associated University Presses, 2002.

MUSLIM-CHRISTIAN RELATIONS

Brog, David. *Standing with Israel,* Frontline, Lake Nary, 2006.

Chafetz, Zev. *A Match Made in Heaven,* Harper Collins, 2007.

Fallaci, Oriana. *The Rage and the Pride,* Rizzoli International Publishers, New York, 2002.

Hagee, John. *Jerusalem Countdown: Updated*, Frontline, 2007.

Israeli, Raphael. *Green Crescent over Nazareth: The Displacement of Christians by Muslims in the Holy Land*, Frank Cass, Portland, 2002.

Ye'or, Bat. *The Decline of Eastern Christianity under Islam*, Associated University Presses, 1996.

Ye'or. Bat and Maisel, David. *The Dhimmi: Jews and Christians under Islam*, Fairleigh Dickinson University Press, 1985.

MUSLIM-JEWISH RELATIONS

Katsh, Abraham I. *Judaism and the Koran*, A.S. Barnes & Co, New York, 1962.

Lewis, Bernard. *The Jews of Islam*, Princeton Univ. Press, 1984.

Lewis, Bernard. *Cultures in Conflict: Christians, Muslims and Jews in the Age of Discovery*, Oxford Univ. Press, 1995.

Nettlerm, Ronald L. (Ed.) *Medieval and Modern Perspectives on Muslim-Jewish Relations*, Harwood, Oxford, 1995.

Stillman, Norman A. *The Jews in Arab Lands: A History and Source Book*, Jewish Publication Society of America, Philadelphia, 1979.

Stillman, Norman A. *The Jews in Arab Lands in Modern Times*, Jewish Publication Soc. of America, Philadelphia, 1991.

ZIONISM

Chertoff, Mordecai (Ed). *Zionism: A Basic Reader,* Herzl Press, New York, 1975.

Edelhelt, Abraham and Hershel. *History of Zionism: A Handbook and Dictionary,* Westview Press, Boulder, Colorado, 2000.

Elon, Amos. *Herzl,* Holt, Rinehardt, Winston, New York, 1975.

Hertzberg, Arthur (Ed*). The Zionist Idea: A Historical Analysis and Reader,* Atheneum, New York, 1972.

Laqueur, Walter. *A History of Zionism,* Holt, Rinehart & Winston, New York, 1972.

Learsi, Rufus. *Fulfillment: The Epic Story of Zionism,* Herzl Press, New York, 1972.

Lowenthal, Marvin (Ed). *The Diaries of Theodor Herzl,* Grosset and Dunlap, New York, 1962.

Troy, Gil. *Why I am a Zionist: Israel, Jewish Identity and the Challenges of Today,* Bronfman Jewish Education Center, Montreal, 2002.

Weizmann, Chaim. *Trial and Error, The Autobiography of Chaim Weizmann,* Schocken Books, New York, 1966.

THE ARAB WORLD & ARAB NATIONALISM (General)

_____. *Arabian Personalities of the Early Twentieth Century,* Oleander Press, New York, 1986.

Agwani, M.S. *Communism in the Arab East,* Asia Publishing House, New York, 1969.

Ajami, Fouad. *The Arab Predicament: Arab Political Thought and Practice since 1967,* Cambridge Univ. Press, 1993.

Ajami, Fouad. *The Dream Palace of the Arabs,* Pantheon Book, New York, 1998.

Bates, Daniel and Rassam, Amal. *Peoples and Cultures of the Middle East,* Prentice-Hall, Englewood Cliffs, N.J. 1983.

Be'eri, Eliezer. *Army Officers in Arab Politics and Society,* Israel Universities Press, Jerusalem, 1969.

Carmichael, Joel. *Arabs Today,* Anchor Press, New York, 1977.

Farah, Tawfic (Ed). *Pan-Arabism and Arab Nationalism: The Continuing Debate,* Westview Press, Boulder, CO., 1987.

Glubb, John Bagot. *Glubb Pasha: A Soldier with the Arabs,* Hodder and Stoughton, London, 1957.

Glubb, John Bagot. *The Great Arab Conquests,* Quarter Books, London, 1963.

Haddad, George M. *Revolutions and Military Rule in the Middle East, Vol. 1- The Northern Tier,* Robert Speller & Sons, New York, 1965.

Haddad, George M. *Revolutions and Military Rule in the Middle East, Vol. 2- The Arab States Part I–Iraq, Syria, Lebanon and Jordan,* Robert Speller & Sons, New York, 1971.

Haddad, George M. *Revolutions and Military Rule in the Middle East, Vol. 3- The Arab States Part 2-Egypt,* the Sudan, Yemen and Libya, Robert Speller & Sons, New York, 1973.

Halliday, Fred. *Arabia without Sultans,* Vintage Books, New York, 1975.

Hatem, M. Abdel Kader. *Information and the Arab Cause,* Longman, London, 1974.

Hitti, Philip K. *The Arabs: A short History,* Regency Publishing, Washington DC, 1996.

Hourani, Albert. *A History of the Arab Peoples,* MF Books, New York, 1991.

Khadduri, Majid. *Arab Contemporaries: The Role of Personalities in Politics,* John Hopkins University Press, Baltimore, 1973.

Kiernan, Thomas. *Arafat The Man and the Myth,* W. Norton, New York, 1976.

Laffin, John. *The Arabs as Master Slavers,* SBS Publishing, Englewood, N.J., 1982.

Landay, Jerry. *Dome of the Rock,* Newsweek, New York, 1972.

Lewis, Bernard. *The Arabs in History,* Oxford University Press, New York, 1993.

Lewis, Bernard. *The Assassins,* Weidenfeld & Nicolson, London, 1967.

Lewis, Bernard. *The Jews of Islam,* Princeton U Press, 1984.

Maalouf, Amin. *The Crusades through Arab Eyes,* Schocken Books, New York, 1985.

Mansfield, Peter. *The Arabs,* Penguin Books, New York, 1983.

Mansfield, Peter. *The Arab World: A Comprehensive History,* Thomas Crowell, New York. 1976.

Patai, Raphael. **The Arab Mind,** Charles Scribners, New York, 1973.

Pryce-Jones, David. **The Closed Circle: An Interpretation of the Arabs,** Harper Collins, 1989.

Quandt, William, Jabber, Fuad and Lesch, Ann. **The Politics of Palestinian Nationalism,** University of California Press, Berkeley, 1973.

EGYPT

Gershoni, Israel. *The Emergence of Pan-Arabism in Egypt,* Shiloah Center for Middle Eastern and African Studies, Tel Aviv, 1981.

Heikal, Mohamed. *The Cairo Documents: The Inside Story of Nasser and His Relationship with World Leaders, Rebels and Statesmen,* Doubleday, New York, 1973.

Hopkins, Harry. *Egypt the Crucible: The Unfinished Revolution in the Arab World,* Houghton Mifflin, Boston, 1969.

Nutting, Anthony. *Nasser,* E.P. Dutton, New York, 1972.

Stephens, Robert. *Nasser: A Political Biography,* Simon and Schuster, New York, 1971.

Vatikiotis, P.J. *The History of Egypt: From Muhammad to Sadat*, Johns Hopkins University Press, Baltimore, 1980.

IRAQ

Al-Khalil, Samir. *Republic of Fear*, Pantheon Books, New York, 1990.

Allawi, Ali. *The Occupation of Iraq: Winning the War, Losing the Peace*, Yale University Press, 2007.

Ghassemlou, A.R., et al. *People without a Country: The Kurds and Kurdistan*, Zed Press, London, 1980.

Khadduri, Majid and Chareeb, Edmund. *War in the Gulf 1990-91: The Iraq-Kuwait Conflict and Its Implications*, Oxford University Press, New York, 1997.

O'Ballance, Edgar. *The Kurdish Struggle, 1920-94*, Palgrave Macmillan, 1996.

O'Ballance, Edgar. *The Kurdish Revolt, 1961-72*, Archon Books, 1973.

JORDAN

Faddah, Mohammad. *The Middle East In Transition: A Study of Jordan's Foreign Policy*, Asia Publishing House, New York, 1974.

Schechtman, Joseph. *Jordan: A State That Never Was*, Cultural Publishing, New York, 1968.

Sinai, Anne and Pollack, Allen (Eds.). *The Hashemite Kingdom of Jordan and the West Bank: A Handbook,* American Academic Association for Peace in the Middle Eat, New York, 1977.

Snow, Peter. *Hussein: A Biography,* Robert Luce, Washington, D.C., 1972.

LEBANON

O'Ballance, Edgar. *Civil War in Lebanon, 1975-92,* Palgrace Macmillan, 2002.

Vocke, Harald. *The Lebanese War: Its Origins and Political Dimensions,* St. Martin's Press, New York, 1978..

Weinberger, Naomi. *Syrian Intervention in Lebanon,* Oxford University Press, New York, 1986.

LIBYA

Cooley, John. *Libyan Sandstorm: The Complete Account of Qaddafi's Revolution,* Holt, Rinehart and Winston, New York, 1982.

First, Ruth. **Libya:** *The Elusive Revolution,* Penguin Books, New York, 1974.

PERSIAN GULF EMIRATES

_____. *Area Handbook for the Peripheral States of the Arabian Peninsula,* Stanford Research Institute, Superintendent of Documents, Washington, D.C., 1971.

Khalifa, Ali Mohammed. *The United Arab Emirates: Unity in Fragmentation,* Westview Press, Boulder, CO., 1979.

Long, David E. *The Persian Gulf,* Westview Press, Boulder, CO., 1976.

THE PALESTINIAN ARABS

Becker, Jillian. *The PLO: The Rise and fall of the Palestine Liberation Organization,* Weidenfeld and Nciolson, London, 1984.

Harkabi, Yehoshafat. *The Palestinian Covenant and its Meaning,* Vallentine Mitchell, London, 1979.

Laffin, John. *The P.L.O. Connections,* Corgi Books, London, 1983.

Livingstone, Neil and Halevy, David. *Inside the PLO,* William Morrow, New York, 1990.

Rubenstein, Danny. *The Mystery of Arafat,* Steerforth Press, South Royalton, VT., 1995.

Rubin, Barry. *Revolution until Victory: the politics and history of the PLO,* Harvard Univ. Press, 1994.

Shemesh, Moshe. *The Palestinian Entity 1959-1974: Arab Politics and the PLO,* Frank Cass, 1988.

SAUDI ARABIA

Baer, Robert. *Sleeping With The Devil: How Washington Sold Out Our Soul for Saudi Crude,* Crown Publishers, New York, 2003.

Emerson, Steven. *The American House of Saud: The Secret Petrodollar Connection,* Franklin Watts, New York, 1985.

Gold, Dore. *Hatred's Kingdom, How Saudi Arabia Supports the New Global Terrorism*, Regnery, Washington, D.C. 2003.

Kelly, J.B. *Arabia, the Gulf and the West*, Basic Books, New York, 1980.

Lindey, Gene. *Saudi Arabia*, Hippocrene, New York, 1991.

Mackey, Sandra. *The Saudis: Inside the Desert Kingdom*, Houghton Mifflin, Boston, 1987.

SOMALIA

Farer, Tom. *War Clouds on the Horn of Africa: The Widening Storm*, Second Edition, Carnegie Endowment for International Peace, New York, 1979.

SUDAN

Holt, P.M. and Daly, M.W. *A History of the Sudan: From the Coming of Islam to the Present Day*, Fifth Edition, Pearson Education, Harlow, England, 2000.

Nelson, Harold et al. *Area Handbook for the Democratic Republic of the Sudan*, Superintendent of Documents, Washington, D.C., 1973.

O'Ballance, Edgar. *Sudan, Civil War and Terrorism, 1956-99*, Palgrave Macmillan, 2000.

SYRIA

Maoz, Moshe. *Asad: The Sphinx of Damascus*, Weidenfeld and Nicolson, New York, 1988.

Rubin, Barry. *The Truth about Syria*, Palgrave-Macmillan, New York, 2007.

Sinai, Anne and Pollack, Allen (Eds.). *The Syrian Arab Republic: A Handbook*, American Academic Association for Peace in the Middle Eat, New York, 1976.

YEMEN

Nyrop, Richard et al. *Area Handbook for the Yemens*, Superintendent of Documents, Washington, D.C., 1977.

O'Ballance, Edgar. *War in the Yemen*, Archon Books, Hamden, CT., 1971.

Schmidt, Dana Adams. *Yemen: The Unknown War*, Holt, Rinehart and Winston, New York, 1968.

Stookey, Robert. *Yemen: The Politics of the Yemen Arab Republic*, Westview Pres, Boulder, CO., 1978.

FOREIGN POWERS IN THE MIDDLE EAST

Arens, Moshe. *Broken Covenant: American Foreign Policy and he Crisis between the U.S. and Israel*, Simon and Schuster, New York, 1995.

Ball, George and Ball, Douglas. *The Passionate Attachment: America's Involvement with Israel 1947 to the Present*, W.W. Norton, New York, 1992.

Bass, Warren. *Support Any Friend: Kennedy's Middle East and the Making of the U.S.-Israel Alliance*, Oxford University Press, New York, 2003.

Beckman, Morris. *The Jewish Brigade: An Army with Two Masters, 1944-1945*, Sarpedon, Rockville Center, New York, 1998.

Blitzer, Wolf. *Between Washington and Jerusalem: A Reporter's Notebook*, Oxford University Press, 1985.

Brands, H.W. *Into the Labyrinth: The United States and the Middle East, 1945-1993*, McGraw Hill, New York, 1994.

Bullard, Reader. *Britain and the Middle East: From Earliest Times to 1963*, Hutchinson University Library, London, 1964.

Confino, M. and Shamir, S. (Ed). *The USSR and the Middle East*, Israel Universities Press, Jerusalem, 1973.

Copeland, Miles. *The Game of Nations*, Simon and Schuster, New York, 1969.

Deutschkron, Inge. *Bonn and Jerusalem: The Strange Coalition*, Chilton Books, Philadelphia, PA., 1970.

Dowty, Alan. *Middle East Crisis: U.S. Decision Making in 1958, 1970, and 1973*, University of California Press, Berkeley, CA. 1984.

Gilbert, Martin. *Churchill and the Jews*, Henry Holt, New York, 2007.

Gold, Dore. *The Fight for Jerusalem*, Regnery, Washington, D.C. 2007.

Hanson, Victor Davis. *Carnage and Culture: Landmark Battles in the Rise to Western Power*, Anchor, 2002.

Heikal, Mohamed. *The Sphinx and the Commissar: The Rise and fall of Soviet Influence in the Middle East,* Harper and Row, New York, 1978.

Hirschmann, Ira. *Red Star Over Bethlehem: Russia Drives to Capture the Middle East,* Simon and Schuster, New York, 1971.

Katz, Mark. *Russia and Arabia: Soviet Foreign Policy toward the Arabian Peninsula,* Johns Hopkins University Press, Baltimore, 1986.

Kuniholm, Bruce. *The Origins of the Cold War in the Near East: Great Power Conflict and Diplomacy in Iran, Turkey, and Greece,* Princeton University Press, Princeton, N.J., 1980.

Laqueur, Walter. *The Struggle for the Middle East: The Soviet Union and the Middle East 1958-1970,* Penguin Books, Baltimore, 1972.

Lederer, Ivo and Vucinich, Wayne (Eds.). *The Soviet Union and the Middle East: The Post World War II Era,* Hoover Institution Press, Stanford, CA. 1974.

Lewis, Bernard. *What went wrong? Western Impact and Middle Eastern Response,* Oxford University Press, New York, 2002.

Oren, Michael B. *Power, Faith, and Fantasy: America in the Middle East 1776 to the Present.* W.W. Norton, New York, 2007.

Pennar, Jaan. *The USSR and the Arabs: The Ideological Dimension, 1917-1972,* Crane, Russak and Company, New York, 1973.

Pryce-Jones, David. *Betrayal: France the Arabs and the Jews,* Encounter Books, New York, 2006.

Quandt, William. *Decade of Decisions: American Policy toward the Arab-Israeli Conflict, 1967-1976*, University of California Press, Berkeley, CA. 1977.

Sacher, Howard. *Europe Leaves the Middle East 1936-1954*, Allen Lane, London, 1974.

Sacher, Howard. *Israel and Europe: An Appraisal in History*, Vintage Books, New York, 1998.

Shaked, Haim and Rabinovich, Itamar (Eds.). *The Middle East and the United States: Perceptions and Policies*, Transaction Books, New Brunswick, NJ, 1980.

Shwadran, Benjamin, *The Middle East, Oil, and the Great Powers*, John Wiley and Sons, New York, 1974.

Smolansky, Oleg. *The Soviet Union and the Arab East Under Khrushchev*, Associated University Presses, Cranbury, N.J., 1974.

Spiegel, Steven. *The Other Arab-Israeli Conflict: Making America's Middle East Policy from Truman to Reagan*, University of Chicago Press, Chicago, 1985.

20th CENTURY MIDDLE EAST

Friedman, Isaiah. *The Question of Palestine 1914-1918: British-Jewish-Arab Relations*, Schocken Books, New York, 1973.

Knox, D. Edward. *The Making of a New Eastern Question: British Palestine Policy and the Origins of Israel, 1917-1925*, Catholic University of America Press, Washington, D.C., 1981.

Mack, John. *A Prince of Our Disorder: The Life of T.E. Lawrence*, Little, Brown and Company, Boston, 1976.

Sachar, Howard. *The Emergence of the Middle East 1914-1924*, Allen Lane, London, 1970.

Trevelyan, Hunphrey. *The Middle East in Revolution*, Gambit, Boston, 1970.

Van Paasen, Pierre. *The Forgotten Ally*, Top Executive Media, 2005.

Weber, Frank G. *The Evasive Neutral: Germany, Britain and the Quest for a Turkish Alliance in the Second World War*, University of Missouri Press, Columbia, MO, 1979.

Westwood, John. *The History of the Middle East Wars*, World Publications, North Dighton, MA. 2002.

Yergin, Daniel. *The Prize: The Epic Quest for Oil, Money and Power*, Simon and Schuster, New York 1991.

ISRAEL (General)

Avriel, Ehud. *Open the Gates! A Personal Story of the "Illegal" Immigration to Israel*, Atheneum, New York, 1975.

Benziman, Uzi. *Sharon, An Israeli Caesar*, Adama Books, New York, 1985.

Bruce, F.F. *Carta's Bible History Atlas*, Carta, Jerusalem. 1982.

Cohen, Avner. *Israel and the Bomb*, Columbia University Press, New York, 1998..

Correspondents of the New York Times, *Israel: The Historical Atlas*, New York, 1997.

Dayan. Moshe. *Moshe Dayan: Story of My Life*, William Morrow, New York, 1976.

Derogy, Jacques and Carmel, Hesi. *The Untold History of Israel*, Grove Press, New York, 1979.

Dershowitz, Alan. *The Case for Israel*, Wiley & Sons, 2003.

Eisenberg, Dennis, Dan, Uri, et al. *The Mossad: Inside Stories*, Paddington Press, New York, 1978.

Elon, Amos. *Jerusalem: Battlegrounds of Memory*, Kodansha International, New York, 1995.

Evron, Yair. *Israel's Nuclear Dilemma*, Cornell University Press, Ithaca, N.Y., 1994.

Gilbert, Martin. *Exile and Return: The Emergence of Jewish Statehood*, Steimatzky's Agency, Jerusalem, 1978.

Gilbert, Martin. *Israel: A History*, William Morrow, New York, 1998.

Gilbert, Martin. *Jerusalem: Rebirth of a City*, Viking Press, New York, 1985.

Gilbert, Martin. *Jerusalem in the Twentieth Century*, Wiley, 1996.

Gordis, Daniel. *If a Place can Make You Cry: Dispatches from an Anxious State*, Crown Publishers, New York, 2002.

Herzog, Chaim. *Heroes of Israel: Profiles of Jewish Courage*, Little, Brown and Company, Boston, 1989.

Hillel, Shlomo. *Operation Babylon*, Collins, London, 1988.

Holly, David C. *Exodus, 1947,* Revised Edition, Naval Institute Press, Annapolis, MD., 1995.

Katz, Samuel. *Soldier Spies: Israeli Military Intelligence,* Presidio, Novato, CA, 1992.

Katz, Shmuel. *Battletruth: The World and Israel,* Dvir, Tel Aviv, 1983.

Karsh, Efraim. *Fabricating Israeli History: The New Historians,* Frank Cass, London, 2000.

Kollek, Teddy and Pearlman, Moshe. *Jerusalem: Sacred City of Mankind, a History of Forty Centuries,* Steinmatzky's Agency, Jerusalem, 1968.

Kurzman, Dan. *Ben-Gurion: Prophet of Fire,* Simon and Schuster, New York, 1983.

Lau-Lavie, Naphtali. *Moshe Dayan: A Biography,* Hartmore House, Hartford, 1968.

Mann, Peggy. *Golda: The Life of Israel's Prime Minister,* Coward, McCann, and Geoghagen, New York, 1971.

Meir, Golda. *My Life,* G. Putnam, New York, 1975.

Miller, Anita. Miller, Jordan & Zetouni, Sigalit. *Sharon: Israel's Warrior-Politician,* Academy Chicago Publishing, 2002.

Naggar, David. *The Case for a Larger Israel,* Deje Publishing, San Francisco, 2007.

Netanyahu, Benjamin. *A Place Among the Nations: Israel and the World,* Bantam Books, New York, 1993.

Perlmutter, Amos. *The Life and Times of Menachem Begin*, Doubleday & Company, New York, 1987.

Perry, Dan and Ironside, Alfred. *Israel at Fifty*, General Publishing Group, Santa Monica, CA. 1996.

Rabin, Yitzhak. *The Rabin Memoirs*, Little, Brown, Boston, 1979.

Rabinovich, Itamar & Reinharz, Yehuda (Eds.), *Israel in Middle East, Documents and Readings on Society Politics and Foreign Relations 1948-1984*, Oxford Univ. Press, 1984

Raviv, Dan and Melman, Yossi. *Every Spy a Prince: The Complete History of Israel's Intelligence Community*, Houghton Mifflin, Boston, 1990.

Rosenthal, Monroe and Mozeson, Isaac. *Wars of the Jews: A Military History from Biblical to Modern Times*, Hippocrene Books, New York, 1990.

Sachar, Howard. *A History of Israel: From the Rise of Zionism to Our Time*, 2nd Edition, Alfred Knopf, New York. 1996.

Thomas, Gordon. *Gideon's Spies: the Secret History of the Mossad*, Thomas Dunn Books, New York, 1999.

Thubron, Thomas. *Jerusalem*, Time-Life Books, Amsterdam, 1976.

Wasserstein, Bernard. *Divided Jerusalem*, Yale Univ. Press, 2002.

ISRAEL'S FOREIGN POLICY

Brecher, Michael. *Decisions in Israel's Foreign Policy*, Yale University Press, New Haven, 1975.

Brecher, Michael. *The Foreign Policy System of Israel*, Yale University Press, New Haven, 1972.

Carol, Steven. *From Jerusalem to the Lion of Judah and beyond: Israel's Foreign Policy in East Africa since 1948*, 2008.

Curtis, Michael and Gitelson, Susan (Eds.). *Israel and the Third World*, Transaction Books, New Brunswick, N.J., 1976.

Dagan, Avigdor. *Moscow and Jerusalem: Twenty Years of Relations between Israel and the Soviet Union*, Abelard-Schuman, London, 1970.

Klieman, Aaron. *Israel's Global Reach: Arms Sales as Diplomacy*, Pergammon Books, Washington, D.C., 1985.

Parfitt, Tudor. *Operation Moses: The Untold Story of the Secret Exodus of the Falasha Jews from Ethiopia*, Stein and Day, New York, 1985.

Rafael, Gideon. *Destination Peace: Three Decades of Israeli Foreign Policy*, Stein and Day, New York, 1981.

THE ARAB-ISRAEL CONFLICT (General)

Allon, Yigal. *Shield of David: The Story of Israel's Armed Forces*, Weidenfeld and Nicolson, London, 1970.

Anbar, Michael. *Israel and its Future: Analysis and Suggestions*, iUniverse, Inc., New York, 2004.

Bard, Mitchell. *Myths and Facts: A Guide to the Arab-Israeli Conflict* American-Israel Cooperative Enterprise, Chevy Chase, Md., 2002.

Bartov, Hanoch. *Dado: 48 Years and 20 Days,* Ma'ariv Book Guild, 1981.

Bauer, Yehuda. *From Diplomacy to Resistance: A History of Jewish Palestine, 1939-1945,* Atheneum, New York, 1973.

Ben-Zohar, Michael. *Spies in the Promised Land,* Houghton Mifflin, Boston, 1972.

Betser, Muki. *Secret Soldier: The True Life Story of Israel's Greatest Commando,* Atlantic Monthly Press, New York, 1996.

Cohen, Eliezer. *Israel's Best Defense,* Orion Books, New York, 1993.

Eitan, Raful. *A Soldier's Story: The Life and Times of an Israeli War Hero,* Shapolsky Publishing, New York, 1991.

Elazar, Daniel J. (Ed). *Judea, Samaria and Gaza: Views on the Present and the Future,* American Enterprise Institute, Washington, D.C., 1982.

Gervasi, Frank. *The Case for Israel,* Viking Press, New York, 1967.

Gilbert, Martin. *Historical Atlas of the Arab-Israeli Conflict,* Routledge, New York, 7th edition, 2002.

Griess, Thomas (Ed). *The West Point Military History Series: Atlas of The Arab-Israeli Wars, The Chinese Civil War, and the Korean War,* Avery Publishing, Wayne, N.J., 1987.

Griess, Thomas (Ed). ***The West Point Military History Series: The Arab-Israeli Wars, The Chinese Civil War, and the Korean War,*** Avery Publishing, Wayne, N.J., 1987.

Harkabi, Yehoshafat. *Arab Attitudes towards Israel*, Israel Universities Press, Jerusalem, 1972.

Harkabi, Yehoshafat. *Palestinians and Israel*, John Wiley and Sons, New York, 1974.

Harkabi, Yehoshafat. *Israel's Fateful Decision*, Harper & Row, New York, 1989.

Hersh, Seymour. *The Samson Option: Israel, America and the Bomb*, Faber and Faber, London, 1991.

Herzog, Chaim. *The Arab-Israeli Wars*, Random House, New York, 1982.

Ingrams, Doreen. *Palestine Papers 1917-1922: Seeds of Conflict*, George Braziller, New York, 1972.

Katz, Samuel. *Battleground: Fact and Fantasy in Palestine*, Revised Edition, Taylor Productions, New York, 2002.

Karetzky, Stephen. & Frankel Norman. (Eds.), *The Media Coverage of the Arab-Israeli Conflict*, Shapolsky Publishers, New York, 1989.

Laqueur, Walter. *The Israel-Arab Reader: A Documentary History of the Middle East Conflict*, Seventh Edition, Bantam Books, New York, 2008.

Levin, Kenneth. *The Oslo Syndrome*, Smith & Kraus, 2005.

Lorch, Netanel. *One Long War: Arab versus Jew since 1920*, Keter, Jerusalem, 1976.

Moore, John N. (Ed). *The Arab-Israeli Conflict: Readings and Documents,* Princeton University Press, Princeton, N.J., 1977.

Narrett, Eugene. *Gathered Against Jerusalem,* Writers Club Press, 2000.

O'Brien, Conor Cruse. *The Siege,* Simon and Schuster, New York, 1986.

Parkes, James. *Whose Land? A History of the Peoples of Palestine,* Penguin Books, New York, 1970.

Peters, Joan. *From Time Immemorial: The Origins of the Arab-Jewish Conflict over Palestine,* Harper & Row, New York, 1984.

Prittie, Terence and Nelson, Walter H. *The Economic War against the Jews,* Congi Books, London, 1979.

Rosenfeld, Alvin. *The Plot To Destroy Israel: The Road to Armageddon,* G. P. Putnam's Sons, New York, 1977.

Sharon, Ariel with Chanoff, David. *Warrior: The Autobiography of Ariel Sharon,* Simon and Schuster, New York, 1989.

Shem-Ur, Ora. *The Challenges of Israel,* Shengold Publishers, New York, 1980.

Sykes, Christopher. *Crossroads to Israel: 1917-1948,* Indiana University Press, Bloomington, IN., 1973.

Tessler, Mark. *A History of the Israeli-Palestinian Conflict,* Indiana University Press, Bloomington, IN., 1994.

Van Creveld. *The Sword and the Olive: A Critical History of the Israeli Defense Force,* Public Affairs Press, New York, 1998.

ISRAELI WAR OF INDEPENDENCE & ITS AFTERMATH

Begin, Menachem. *The Revolt,* Nash Publishing, New York, 1977.

Bell, John Bowyer. *Terror out of Zion: Irrgun Zvai Leuni, LEHI, and the Palestine Underground, 1929-1949,* St. Martin's Press, New York, 1977.

Bercusson, David. *The Secret Army.* Stein and Day, New York, 1984.

Berkman, Ted. *Cast A Giant Shadow,* Pocketbooks, New York, 1962.

Collins, Larry and Lapierre, Dominique. *O Jerusalem,* Simon and Schuster, New York, 1972.

Gitlin, Jan. *The Conquest of Acre Fortress,* Hadar Publishing House, Tel Aviv, 1968.

Kagan, Benjamin. *The Secret Battle for Israel,* World Publishing, Cleveland, 1986.

Kurzman, Dan. *Genesis 1948: The First Arab-Israeli War,* World Publishing, New York, 1970.

Larkin, Margaret. *The Six Days of Yad Mordechai,* Yad Mordechai Museum, Givatayim, Israel, 1976.

Lorch, Netanel. *The Edge of the Sword: Israel's War of Independence, 1947-1949,* G.P. Putnam's Sons, New York, 1961.

Milstein, Uri. *History of the War of Independence Vol. I: A Nation Girds for War,* University Press of America, Lanham, MD, 1996.

Milstein, Uri. *History of the War of Independence Vol. II: The First Month*, University Press of America, Lanham, MD, 1997.

Milstein, Uri. *History of the War of Independence Vol. III: The First Invasion*, University Press of America, Lanham, MD, 1998.

Milstein, Uri. *History of the War of Independence Vol. IV: Out of Crisis Came Decision*, University Press of America, Lanham, MD, 1998.

Morris, Benny. *Israel's Border Wars 1949-1956*, Oxford University Press, New York, 1993.

O'Ballance, Edgar. *The Arab-Israeli War, 1948-49*, Hyperion Press, 1983.

Sharef, Zeev. *Three Days*, Doubleday, Garden City, N.Y., 1962.

Slater, Leonard. *The Pledge*, Simon and Schuster, New York, 1970.

Teveth, Shabtai. *Ben Gurion and the Palestinian Arabs: From Peace to War*, Oxford University Press, New York, 1985.

THE SINAI-SUEZ WAR & ITS AFTERMATH

Bowie, Robert. *Suez 1956, International Crisis and the Rule of Law*, Oxford University Press, New York 1974.

Dayan, Moshe. *Diary of the Sinai Campaign*, Schocken Books, New York, 1966.

Eden, Anthony. *The Suez Crisis of 1956*, Beacon Press, Boston, 1960.

Georges-Picot, Jacques. *The Real Suez Crisis,* Harcourt, Brace, Jovanovich, New York, 1978.

Golan, Aviezer. *Operation Susannah,* Harper and Row, New York, 1978.

Henriques, Robert. *100 Hours to Suez,* Pyramid Books, New York, 1957.

Lotz, Wolfgang. *The Champagne Spy,* St. Martin's Press, New York, 1972.

Neff, Donald. *Warriors at Suez,* Linden Press, New York, 1981.

O'Ballance, Edgar. *The Sinai Campaign, 1956,* Frederick A. Praeger, 1960.

Shucjburgh, Evelyn. *Descent to Suez: Diaries 1951-56,* Weidenfeld and Nicolson, London, 1986.

Thomas, Hugh. *Suez,* Harper & Row, New York, 1967.

Troen, S.I. and Shemesh, M. (Eds.). *The Suez-Sinai Crisis, 1956: Retrospective and Reappraisal,* Columbia University Press, New York, 1990.

THE SIX DAY WAR & ITS AFTERMATH

Churchill, Randolph and Winston S. *The Six Day War,* Heinemann, London, 1970.

Cristol, A. Jay. *The Liberty Incident: The 1967 Israeli Attack on the U.S. Navy Spy Ship,* Brassey's, Inc., Washington, D.C. 2002.

Eisenberg, Dennis, Landau, Eli and Portugali, Menachem. *Operation Uranium Ship,* Steimatzky, Tel Aviv, 1978.

Karpin, Michael. *The Bomb in the Basement: How Israel went nuclear and what that means for the world*, Simon & Schuster, New York, 2006.

Kosut, Hal (Ed). *Israel and the Arabs: The June 1967 War*, Facts on File, New York, 1968.

Laqueur, Walter. *The Road to War: The Origin and Aftermath of the Arab-Israeli Conflict 1967-8*, Penguin Books, Baltimore, Maryland, 1968.

Marshall, S.L.A. *Swift Sword: the Historical Record of Israel's Victory, June, 1967*, American Heritage Publishing. 1967.

Moskin, J. Robert. *Among Lions: The Definitive Account of the 1967 Battle for Jerusalem*, Arbor House, New York, 1982.

Neff, Donald. *Warriors for Jerusalem: The Six Days that Changed the Middle East*, Linden Press, New York, 1984.

O'Ballance, Edgar. *The Third Arab-Israeli War, 1967*, Archon Books, 1972.

Oren, Michael B. *Six Days of War: June 1967 and the Making of the Modern Middle East*, Oxford University Press, New York, 2002.

Pryce-Jones, David. *The Face of Defeat: Palestinian Refugees and Guerrillas*, Holt, Rinehart and Winston, New York, 1972.

Rabinovich, Abraham. *The Boats of Cherbourg*, Seaver Books, New York, 1988.

Safran, Nadav. *From War to War: The Arab-Israeli Confrontation 1948-1967*, Pegasus, New York, 1969.

Stevenson, William. *Strike Zion!,* Bantam Books, New York, 1967.

Velie, Lester. *Countdown in the Holy Land,* Funk and Wagnalls, New York, 1969.

THE 1000 DAY WAR OF ATTRITION

Bar-Siman-Tov, Yaacov. *The Israel-Egyptian War of Attrition, 1969-1970: A Case-Study of Limited Local War,* Columbia University Press, 1980.

O'Ballance, Edgar. *The Electronic War in the Middle East, 1968-70,* Shoe String Press, 1974.

O'Neill, Bard E. *Revolutionary Warfare in the Middle East: The Israelis vs. the Fedayeen,* Paladin Press, Boulder, Colorado, 1974.

THE YOM KIPPUR/RAMADAN WAR & ITS AFTERMATH

Adan, Avraham. *The Yom Kippur War,* Drum Books, New York, 1986.

Asher, Jerry. *Duel for the Golan: The 100 Hour Battle that Saved Israel,* William Morrow, New York, 1987.

Ben-Porat, Y., Haber, Eitan and Schiff, Ze'ev. *Entebbe Rescue,* Dell Publishing, New York, 1977.

Boyne, Walter J. *The Two O'clock War,* St. Martin's Press, New York. 2002.

Brecher, Michael. *Decisions in Crisis: Israel, 1967 and 1973,* University of California Press, Berkeley. 1980.

Herzog, Chaim. *The War of Atonement*, Steinmatzky's Agency, Jerusalem, 1975.

Heikal, Mohamed. *The Road to Ramadan*, Quadrangle Books, New York, 1975.

Insight Team of the Sunday Times. *Insight on the Middle East War*, Andre Deutsch, London, 1974.

Katz, Shmuel. *The Hollow Peace*, Dvir, 1981.

Kohler, Foy, Goure, Leon and Harvey, Mose. *The Soviet Union and the October 1973 Middle East War: Implications for Détente*, University of Miami, Miami, 1974.

Laqueur, Walter. *Confrontation: The Middle East and World Politics*, Bantam Books, New York, 1974.

O'Ballance, Edgar. *No Victor, No Vanquished: The Yom Kippur War*, Presidio Press, Rafael, CA., 1978.

Schiff, Ze'ev. *October Earthquake: Yom Kippur 1973*, University Publishing Projects, Tel Aviv, 1974.

Sobel, Lester A. (Ed) *Israel and the Arabs: The October 1973 War*, Facts on File, New York, 1974.

Stevenson, William. *90 Minutes at Entebbe*, Bantam, New York, 1976.

Zodhy, Badri. *The Ramadan War, 1973*, Hippocrene Books, New York, 1979.

THE ISRAEL-PLO WAR IN LEBANON

Israeli, Raphael (Ed). *PLO In Lebanon: Selected Documents*, Weidenfeld and Nicolson, London, 1983.

Landau, Julian. *The Media: Freedom or Responsibility: The War in Lebanon1982, A Case Study*, B.A.L. Mass Communications, Jerusalem, 1984.

Schiff, Ze'ev and Ya'ari, Ehud. ***Israel's Lebanon War***, Simon and Schuster, New York, 1984.

THE ISRAELI STRIKE ON IRAQ'S NUCLEAR FACILITY

Claire, Robert. *Raid on the Sun*, Broadway Books, New York. 2004.

Nakdimon, Shlomo. *First Strike*, Summit Books, New York, 1987.

Weissman, Steve and Krosney, Herbert. *The Islamic Bomb*, NY Times Books, New York, 1981.

IRAN

Graham, Robert. *Iran: The Illusion of Power*, St. Martin's Press, New York, 1979.

Kapuscinski, Ryszard. *Shah of Shahs*, Harcourt, Brace, Jovanovich, New York, 1982.

McCuen, Gary. *Iran-Iraq War*, Gem Publications, Hudson, WI., 1987.

Taheri, Amir. *The Spirit of Allah: Khomeini and the Islamic Revolution*, Adler & Adler, 1986.

Timmerman, Kenneth R. *Countdown to Crisis: The coming Nuclear Showdown with Iran*, New York: Crown Forum, 2005.

TERRORISM AND JIHAD

Bar Zohar, Michael and Haber, Eitan. *The Quest for the Red Prince,* William Morrow, New York, 1983.

Bawer, Bruce. *While Europe Slept: How Radical Islam is destroying the West from Within,* Doubleday, 2006.

Bukay, David. *Mohammad's Monsters,* Ariel Center for Policy Research, 2004.

Dershowitz, Alan M. *Why Terrorism Works: Understanding the Threat, Responding to the Challenge,* Yale Univ. Press, 2002.

Dietl, Wilhelm. *Holy War,* Macmillan, New York, 1984.

Dobson, Christopher. *Black September: Its Short, Violent History,* Macmillan Publishing, New York, 1974.

Dobson, Christopher and Payne, Ronald. *Counterattack: The West's Battle Against the Terrorists,* Facts on File, New York, 1982.

Ehrenfeld, Rachel. *Funding Evil: How terrorism is financed-and how to stop it,* Bonus Books, Chicago, 2003.

Emerson, Steven. *American Jihad: The terrorists living among us,* The Free Press, New York, 2002.

Emerson, Steven. *Jihad Incorporated,* Prometheus, Amherst. 2006.

Firestone, Reuven. *Jihad: The Origin of Holy War in Islam,* Oxford Uni. Press, New York, 1999.

Fregosi, Paul. *Jihad in the West,* Prometheus, Amherst, 1998.

Frumm David & Pearle, Richard. *An End to Evil: How to Win the war on terror,* Random House, 2003.

Gabriel, Brigette. *Because They Hate: A Survivor of Islamic Terror Warns America,* St. Martin's Press, New York, 2006.

Gerges, Fawas A. *Journey of the Jihadist,* Harcourt Books, Orlando, 2006.

Hamid, Tawfik. *The Roots of Jihad,* Top Executive Media, Denver, 2006.

Habeck Mary. *Knowing the Enemy,* Yale University Press, 2006.

Huntington, Samuel P. *The Clash of Civilizations and the Remaking of World Order,* Touchstone, Simon & Schuster, 1996.

Kepel, Illes. *Jihad: The Trail of Political Islam,* Harvard Univ. Press, 2002.

Laqueur, Walter. *No end to War: Terrorism in the Twenty First Century,* Continuum, New York, 2003.

Laqueur, Walter. *The Age of Terrorism,* Little, Brown and Company, Boston, 1987.

Laqueur, Walter. *The New Terrorism,* Oxford University Press, New York, 1999.

Lindsey, Hal. *The Everlasting Hatred: The Roots of Jihad,* Oracle House Publishing, 2002.

Melman, Yossi. *The Master Terrorist: The True Story behind Abu Nidal,* Adama Books, New York, 1986.

Netanyahu, Benjamin. *Fighting Terrorism,* Farrar, Straus, Giroux, New York, 1995.

Netanyahu, Benjamin (Ed). *Terrorism: How The West Can Win.* Farrar, Straus, Giroux, New York. 1986.

Parry, Albert. *Terrorism: From Robespierre to Arafat,* Vanguard Press, New York, 1976.

Pape, Robert A. *Dying to Win,* Random House, 2005.

Peters, Ralph. *Beyond Terror: Strategy in a Changing World,* Stackpole Books, Mechanicburg, PA, 2002.

Phares, Walid. **Future** *Jihad: Terrorist Strategies against America,* Macmillan, 2005.

Phares, Walid. *The Confrontation: Winning the war Against Future Jihad,* Palgrave Macmillan, New York, 2008.

Phillips, Melanie. *Londonistan,* Encounter Books, 2006.

Pipes, Daniel. *Militant Islam Reaches America,* W. W. Norton, New York, 2003.

Poole, John H. *Tactics of the Crescent Moon,* Posterity Press, Emerald Isle, 2004.

Rubin, Barry and Rubin, Judith (Eds.). *Anti-American Terrorism and the Middle East: A Documentary Reader,* Oxford University Press, New York, 2006.

Scheuer, Michael. *Through Our Enemies Eyes: Osama Bin Laden, Radical Islam, and the future of America,* Brassey's Inc., Washington, D.C., 2002.

Schindler, John R. *Unholy Terror: Bosnia, Al-Qa'ida, and the Rise of Global Jihad*, Zenith Press, 2007.

Singer, Saul. *Confronting Jihad*, Cold Spring Press, Cold Spring Harbor, 2003.

Spencer, Robert. *Onward Muslim Soldiers: How Jihad still threatens the West*, Regency Publishing Company, Washington, DC, 2003.

Steyn, Mark. *America Alone: The End of the World As We Know It.* Regnery Publishing, Washington, D.C. 2006.

Timmerman, Kenneth R. *Preachers of Hate: Islam and the War on America*, Crown Forum, New York, Random House, 2003.

THE MOVEMENT TOWARD PEACE

Ben-Meir Alon. *The War We Must Win*, Author House, Bloomington, 2004.

Cohen, Raymond. *Culture and Conflict in Egyptian-Israel Relations: A Dialogue of the Deaf*, Indiana Univ. Press, 1990.

Kimche, Jon. *There Could Have Been Peace*, Dial Press, 1973.

Netanyahu, Benjamin. *A Durable Peace: Israel and Its Place among the Nations.* Warner Books, 2000.

Rabinovich, Itamar. *The Brink of Peace: The Israeli-Syrian Negotiations*, Princeton Univ. Press, 1998.

Rabinovitch, Itamar. *The Road Not Taken: Early Arab-Israeli Negotiations*, Oxford University Press, New York, 1991.

Stone, Julius. *Israel and Palestine: Assault on the Law of Nations,* Johns Hopkins University Press, Baltimore, 1981.

Weizman, Ezer. *The Battle for Peace,* Bantam, New York, 1981.

Internet Resources

MIDDLE EAST (General)

Facts and Logic about the Middle East: http://www.factsandlogic.org/

Flags of the World: http://www.crwflags.com/fotw/flags/

Maps: http://www.jewishvirtuallibrary.org/jsource/History/maptoc.html

Maps–Who Ruled the Middle East: http://www.mapsofwar.com/images/EMPIRE17.swf

MidEast Truth Forum: http://www.mideasttruth.com/

Middle East conflicts: http://www.acig.org/artman/publish/cat_index_22.shtml

Middle East conflicts by nation: http://www.onwar.com/aced/nation/index.htm

Middle East Forum: http://www.meforum.org/

Middle East Radio Forum: www.middleeastradioforum.org

MIDDLE EAST NEWS

Committee for Accuracy in Middle East Reporting in America: www.camera.org

DebkaFile: http://www.debka.com/index.php

Gamla News: http://www.gamla.org.il/english/index.htm

Honest Reporting–Accuracy in the news: www.honestreporting.co

Independent Media Review and Analysis: http://www.imra.org.il/

Israel National News: http://www.israelnationalnews.com/

Jerusalem Post: http://www.jpost.com/

Middle East Media and Research Institute http://www.memri.org

Monitoring the United Nations: http://www.eyeontheun.org/

What is being reported and said in Arab/Muslim press and TV vs. how things are portrayed in our TV, radio and newsprint media–Palestine Media Watch: http://www.pmw.org.il/

ISLAM

Hadith: http://www.imaanstar.com/hadith.php

Monitoring Islam: www.jihadwatch.com

and http://www.jihadwatch.org/dhimmiwatch/

Noble Qur'an (Arabic and English versions available): http://www.imaanstar.com/quran.php

Site run by ex-Muslims: www.faithfreedom.org

Islam Review: http://www.islamreview.com/

Actual presentation and translation of Arab and Iranian state-run TV. Provides comparison to what is presented to Western non-Muslim world: www.memri.org

Searchable Koran with three simultaneous English translations. Created by the Muslim Students Association: www.usc.edu/dept/msa/quran and http://quod.lib.umich.edu/k/koran/

Searchable Hadidth: http://www.usc.edu/dept/MSA/reference/searchhadith.html

Muslim religious website for Muslims: www.islamonline.com Click on Fatwah and Counseling and www.islam-qa.com

DVD Movie "Islam: What the West Needs to Know": www.whatthewestneedstoknow.com

DVD Movie "Obsession: Radical Islam's War against the West": www.obsessionthemovie.com

THE ARAB WORLD

The Arab-Nazi connection: http://www.tellthechildrenthetruth.com/

LEBANON

Free Lebanon: http://www.freelebanon.org/

ZIONISM

Zionism, the first 120 years: http://www.jafi.org.il/education/100/120/7.html

Zionism-Virtual Library: http://www.jewishvirtuallibrary.org/jsource/zion.html

ISRAEL (General)

Arabs for Israel: http://www.arabsforisrael.com/

Ariel Center for Policy Research: http://www.acpr.org.il/

Canada Institute for Jewish Research: http://www.isranet.org/

First Photos of the Holy Land: http://www.eretzyisroel.org/~dhershkowitz/index2.html

Freeman Center for Strategic Studies: http://www.freeman.org/

Historical and Investigative Research: http://www.hirhome.com/

History: http://www.ipi-usa.org/history.htm

International Christian Embassy in Jerusalem: http://www.intournet.co.il/icej

Israel History: http://www.jewishvirtuallibrary.org/jsource/History/ishisttoc.html

Israel media links: http://www.kolisrael.com/

Israeli Security: http://www.iris.org.il/

Israel Virtual Library: http://www.jewishvirtuallibrary.org/jsource/israel.html

Israel's Story in Maps: http://www.israel-mfa.gov.il/MFA/Facts+About+Israel/Israel+in+Maps/Israel+in+Maps.htm

Judea, Samaria and Gaza–the legal case: http://www.israelwhitepaper.org/

Moral Case for Israel: http://www.guardiansofisrael.cheeb.com/moralcase.htm

One Jerusalem: http://www.onejerusalem.org/blog/index.asp

Power Point and Visual Presentations: http://www.ipi-usa.org/presentations.htm

The Temple Mount: http://www.templeinstitute.org/main.htm

The U.S-Israel relationship: http://www.hirhome.com/israel/hirally.htm

THE ARAB-ISRAELI CONFLICT (General)

Conflicts, actions and wars: http://www.onwar.com/aced/nation/ink/israel/findex.htm and http://www.jewishvirtuallibrary.org/jsource/History/wartoc.html

Israeli Air Force at war: http://www.iaf.org.il/Templates/Wars/Wars.aspx?lang=EN&lobbyID=40&folderID=42

Israel Defense Forces History: http://www1.idf.il/DOVER/site/mainpage.asp?sl=EN&srch=&id=5&clr=1

Israel Military History: http://www.israeli-weapons.com/israeli_history.html

Jewish Refugees from Arab and Muslim countries: http://www.theforgottenrefugees.com/index.php?option=com_content&task=view&id=43&Itemid=56

Palestine Facts: http://www.palestinefacts.org/

The Six Day War: http://www.sixdaywar.co.uk/

TERRORISM

Hamas Charter (full text): http://www.frontpagemag.com/Articles/ReadArticle.asp?ID=21029 and

http://www.yale.edu/lawweb/avalon/mideast/hamas.htm

MITP Terrorism Database: http://www.tkb.org/Home.jsp

Terrorism–Virtual Library: http://www.jewishvirtuallibrary.org/jsource/Terrorism/terrortoc.html

THE HOLOCAUST

Educational Holocaust (162) websites are listed: http://www.jr.co.il/hotsites/j-holoc.htm

THE MOVEMENT TOWARDS PEACE

Disengagement: http://www.jafi.org.il/education/actual/conflict/disengagement/index.html

Road to Peace proposal: http://www.therightroadtopeace.com/

Peace Process Virtual Library: http://www.jewishvirtuallibrary.org/jsource/Peace/pptoc.html

About the Author

Dr. Steven Carol has a Ph.D. in History from St. John's University, New York. His specialties are the Modern Middle East, United States history and government, the World Wars of the 20th century and the Cold War.

Now retired, he taught for 38 years both on the East Coast (including Adelphi University and Long Island University) and in Arizona on the High School, College (at Mesa Community College, and Scottsdale Community College) and graduate levels.

He is the author of books, including *From Jerusalem to the Lion of Judah and Beyond: Israel's Foreign Policy in East Africa since 1948*, *Encyclopedia of Days: Start the Day with History,* articles, visual aids, and educational games.

Most recently Dr. Carol has written numerous articles about the Middle East, which have appeared in newspapers in the U.S. and Canada. They have also appeared on the worldwide web at Israel National News, Israpundit, Think-Israel.org, One Jerusalem.org, and the Israel Insider.

Dr. Carol has lectured throughout the United States at churches, synagogues, universities, schools, and service organizations on topics related to the history of the Arab-Israeli conflict, terrorism and about a forgotten rescuer of the Holocaust era, Portuguese diplomat Dr. Aristides de Sousa Mendes.

Dr. Carol, the historian of "The Middle East Radio Forum" (MERF) and Middle East Consultant for the Salem Radio Network, is a frequent guest on the show, providing detailed historical overviews and perspectives frequently relating it to current developments. Additionally, he has been a featured guest on various radio shows across the U.S. and in Israel.

He has been affiliated with the Arizona Humanities Council as part of the "9-11 Conversations" programs, and has spoken on the war on terrorism, and the origins of the Arab-Israeli Conflict among other subjects.

Dr. Carol has also been a consultant for the N.Y. State and Arizona Departments of Education. In 1987, New York State named him "Outstanding Teacher."

INDEX

A

1000 Day War of Attrition 56, 89, 104, 203
14th of Ramadan Revolution 42
Abbasid Caliphate 143
Abu Bakr 138, 142
Abu Musa 91, 155
Abu Nidal organization 51
Acehans 117
Aden 32, 42, 205
Aelia Capitolina 171
Afghanistan 12, 24, 41, 44, 75–76, 95–96, 139, 148, 198
Ahmadinejad, Mahmoud 81
Ahmed Abu Reish Brigade 51
Ahmed I 14
Ahmose I 164
Ainsarii 49
Akhenaton 165
Akkadians 1
Al-Andalus 140
Al-Anfal campaign 44
Al-Aqsa Mosque 13
al-Dura, Muhammad 79
al-insan al-kamil 162
Alamut 50
Alexander the Great 103
Alexandretta 4, 157
Algeria 2, 12, 29, 36, 43, 45, 96, 167, 205
Algerian Civil War 29, 45
Algiers Agreement 66
Allah 13, 19–21, 25, 72, 84, 130–131, 138, 143, 148–149, 240
Allon plan 61
Al Aqsa Intifada 61, 71–72, 77, 79, 83, 105
Al Aqsa Martyrs Brigades 51
Al Qaeda 26, 51
Amenhotep IV 165
Animists 5, 17, 41
Annapolis Conference 162
Antiochus 103
Arab viii, x–xi, 1, 2–3, 3, 4, 5–18, 23, 30–36, 38–40, 41, 42, 44, 47–53, 55, 58, 60–69, 71, 76–78, 81–83, 91, 94–96, 100, 103–105, 108, 110, 113–114, 116–119, 121–124, 130–132, 140–141, 147–148, 151–152, 167–169, 176, 179, 183–184, 186, 189–190, 192, 196–199, 203, 206, 211–213, 215–217, 219–220, 222, 225, 230–235, 237, 244, 247–248, 251, 254
Arab-African Federation 34
Arabian Peninsula 2, 5, 12, 93, 95–96, 138, 219, 224
Arabian Sea 43, 90
Arabistan 4, 27, 170
Arab Federation 31
Arab Islamic Republic 33
Arab Revolt of 1936-1939 38
Arab Sahel State 34
Arab Socialism 35
Arafat, Yasir 58, 61, 64–65, 71, 123, 125–128
Arizona 119, 253–254

Armenian 5
Armenians 5, 40, 93, 147
Armenian Catholics 5
Armenian Orthodox 5
Assad, Hafez al 28
Assyria 30, 102
Assyrian 10, 102
Aswan High Dam 183–184
Aton 165
Attila Line 74, 109
Attlee, Clement 95
avania 159
Ayyubids 11
Ayyubid Empire 30, 143
Azania 117
Azerbaijan 109, 139
Azeris 5

B

Ba'athism 35
Babri Mosque 14
Babur 14
Babylonia 30
Babylonians 1, 10–11, 15, 177–178
Babylonian Talmud 15
Bab el-Mandeb 1, 90
Bahais 5
Bahrain 2–3, 46, 96, 167, 193, 205
Balfour Declaration vii, 22, 111, 115–116
Balkans 94, 143
Baluchis 5
Bangladesh 43, 74, 147
Bar Kokhba, Shimon 54, 103, 171
Basilica of St. Mary 13

Basta 68
Battle of
  Badr 137
  Cirmen 144
  Hattin 143
  Karbala 139
  Khaybar 138
  Kosovo 144
  Lepanto 145
  Manzikert 142
  Mohács 145
  Poitiers 12, 141
  Qadisiyya 138
  Varna 144
  Vienna 12, 145
  Yarmuk 138
bazaar diplomacy 63
Beersheba 197
Beirut 68, 143, 209
Berbers 5, 140
Biafra 117
bin Laden, Osama 149
Black September 43, 51, 241
Blue Mosque 14
Böhmen und Mähren 170
Bolton, John 193
Bonaparte, Napoleon 88
Bonhoeffer, Dietrich 84
Bosnian war 45
Bosporus 1, 87, 94
Brazil 189
Bulgaria 49, 93, 107–108, 144
Bunche, Ralph 162
Buraimi Oasis 41
burqa 23
Byzantines 11, 141–142
Byzantine Empire 138, 142, 144

C

Caesar, Julius 166

Caliphate 25, 83, 138–139, 141–142, 144
Camp David 61, 105
Camp David II 61, 105
Caspian Sea 50, 93
Cathedral of St. John the Baptist 13
Cathedral of the Sacred Heart 14
Catherine the Great 145–146
Cave of the Biblical Patriarchs 13
Cenacle 175
Chad 33, 44, 46, 193
Chaldean 5, 10, 30, 102, 177
Chaldean Catholics 5
Chaldean Empire 30
Chamoun, Camille 68
Chechnya 12, 45, 135, 149
Chechnya War 45
Cheops 164
Chirol, Valentine 94
Christianity 1, 141, 149, 151, 213
Christians 14, 17, 20, 40–43, 45, 84, 103, 108, 135, 138, 142–143, 145, 147–149, 152–153, 159–162, 171, 211, 249
Christian Quarter 159
Churchill, Winston 94–95
Church of the Nativity 160
Circassians 5
Clearchus 169
Cleopatra 166
Cold War 37, 224, 253
Comoros 167, 193

Compagnie Universelle du Canal de Suez 88, 186
Constantinople viii, 13, 56, 88, 139–140, 144, 182
Constantinople Convention viii, 56, 88, 182
Coptic Catholics 5
Coptic Orthodox 5
Corpus Separatum 196
Crete 94, 140–141, 146
Crimean War 37
Crusaders 11, 49, 54, 142, 176
Cyprus 3, 42–43, 74, 96, 109, 139, 141, 145, 148, 155, 189
Cyrus the Great 102
Czech Republic 170

D

Damavand Line 74
Dardanelles 1, 87
Darfur 46
darura 65
Dar al-Harb 11, 19
Dar al-Islam 11, 19
Davos Conference 61
Dead Sea 173, 197
Democratic Front for the Liberation of Palestine 51
de Lesseps, Ferdinand 88, 184
dhimmi 63, 72, 159
dhimmitude 19, 144, 159, 162
Dhofar Liberation Front 73
Dhofar Province 42, 73
Diaspora 103, 177, 211
Djibouti 34, 167, 193
Dobruja 108

Dome of the Rock 13, 16, 139, 216
Dormition Abbey 175
Druse 142
Dulles, John Foster 95–96

E

East Timor 148, 155
Eban, Abba 179
Eden, Anthony 186
Egypt viii, x, 2, 28–33, 36, 43, 46, 48, 50, 55–56, 61, 66, 68–69, 76, 88–89, 93–96, 104, 121, 139, 142–144, 155, 163–168, 173, 175, 182–186, 190, 193, 198, 205, 216–218
Egyptians viii, 1, 6, 10–11, 28, 39, 42, 47–50, 52, 55–56, 62, 66, 68–69, 81, 88–90, 101, 165, 182–186, 198, 238, 244
Egyptian Islamic Jihad 52, 69
Eilat 27, 82, 90, 173
Eisenhower, Dwight D. 96
Eisenhower Doctrine 96, 99–100
Elburz mountains 50
Enterprise Passage 90
Epiphanius 171
Eritrea 45, 89, 94, 167
Ethiopia 38, 42, 94–96, 145–146, 192, 198, 230
Euphrates x, 1, 30, 165
Euphrates River 165
European Union 6, 71
Exodus 166, 228, 230
ex injuria jus non oritur 49, 52

F

Fatahland 57
Fatah Constitution vii, 8, 131
Fatamids 142
Fatimid Empire 30
Fedayeen 50–51, 238
Federation of Arab Emirates of the South 32
Federation of Arab Republics 33
Federation of South Arabia 32
Feisal-Weizmann agreement 60
Field of the Blackbirds 144
First Crusade 142
First Lebanese Civil War 68
First Temple 10, 101–102
Force 48, 50, 56–57, 66, 83, 233, 250
Force 17 50
France 3, 12, 36, 79, 116, 140–141, 157, 181, 186, 224
French-Israeli alliance 36

G

Gallipoli 87, 143
Gandhi, Indira 189
Gaza 8, 10, 39, 49–50, 52, 55, 62, 70, 72–73, 79, 81–82, 110–111, 113, 118–119, 121–122, 125–126, 128, 155–157, 173, 197, 231, 250
Gaza Strip 10, 49–50, 52, 55, 62, 81, 111, 113, 121–122, 125, 155–156, 173
Gibraltar 12, 140
Goebbels, Joseph 82

Golan Heights 8, 52, 55, 111, 113, 120, 155–157, 173
Granada 144
Grand Mosque in Mecca 43
Grand Mosque of Damascus 13
Great Arab Revolt of 1916 38
Great Britain 3, 31, 38, 111–113, 156, 181
Greece 53, 87, 93–96, 107, 143–144, 146, 190, 198, 224
Greeks 11, 40, 93, 107, 109, 147, 198
Greek Catholics 5
Greek Orthodox 5
Greek War of Independence 37
Gulf War I 44, 75, 105

H

Hadrian 171
Hagia Sophia 13–14
Halabja 44
Halaieb territory 46
Hama, Syria 44
Hamas Covenant vii, 8, 129
Hammarskjold, Dag 66, 68
Haq al-Auda 18
harbi 17
Hashemites 38
Hashshashin 49
Hatay 27
Hatshepsut 165
Hawari 50
Hawar Islands 46
Hebrews 1
Hebron 13, 27, 67, 104, 127, 196
Hebron Protocol 67, 127
Hegira 137
Hejaz 41, 138

Herod 103
Hershler, Aharon 8
Herzl, Theodor 103
Herzog, Chaim 191
Hezbollah 21, 24, 28, 39–40, 44, 52, 57–58, 70, 80, 105, 149
Hezbollahland 57
Hezekiah 102
hijab 9, 23
Hochberg-Yahrawi understanding 60
Hogarth, Dr. D.G. 93
Holocaust 17, 152, 251, 254
Hormuz 1, 90–91
Hornbeam Line 74
hudna 64, 70
Hulagu Khan 143
Hulda Gate 15
Hungary 49, 53, 108, 144–146, 181
Husayn ibn Ali 139
Hussein, Saddam 28, 31, 42

I

Iberian Peninsula 12, 140
ibn Saud 3
Ibrahimi Mosque 13
India 12–14, 50, 74–75, 94–95, 109, 117, 189, 192, 198
Indonesia 42–43, 117, 148–149, 155
intifada 71, 79, 105
Iran 2, 12, 24, 29, 36, 39–41, 43–44, 47, 50, 58, 66, 72, 76, 90–91, 93–96, 135, 155, 170, 187, 189, 198, 224, 240
Iranian Revolution 39, 51, 83

Iraq 2–3, 12, 24, 31–36, 38, 40–46, 52, 66, 72, 75–77, 90, 94–96, 138–139, 167, 198, 205, 215, 218, 240
Iskenderun 4
Islam vii–viii, x, 1, 5, 10–13, 19–20, 22, 25, 62–63, 65, 83, 123, 129–131, 133, 135, 137–139, 141–142, 148–149, 151, 159, 161, 208–213, 216, 221, 241–244, 247, 248
Islamic Mass Media Charter 78
Islamic Salvation Front 29
Islamic world 9, 40, 70, 78, 130–131
Islamofascism 82–84
Islamofascists 13, 24, 83, 84, 135
Israel vii–viii, x–xii, 2–3, 6–8, 10–12, 15–18, 27, 36, 39–40, 46–53, 55–63, 65–73, 77, 79–80, 82, 96, 101–102, 104–105, 109–111, 113, 117–129, 131, 133, 135, 138, 142, 147, 149, 151, 153, 155–157, 169–171, 173, 176–179, 182, 184, 190–193, 196, 199, 203, 212, 214–215, 217, 222–223, 225–235, 237–240, 244–245, 247, 249–250, 253–254
Israel-Egypt Disengagement Agreement 66
Israel-Jordan Armistice Agreement 151
Israeli War of Independence 83, 104, 151

Istanbul 13
Italy 3, 49, 53, 89, 116, 140–141, 144, 181

J

Jacobite (Syrian) 5
janjaweed 46
Jeddah 84
Jericho 52, 125
Jerusalem viii, 3, 8, 10–11, 13–16, 22, 27, 49, 54–56, 61, 64, 71–72, 77, 82, 101–104, 120, 122, 132, 138–139, 142–143, 147, 151–153, 160–162, 171, 175–179, 196–197, 213, 215, 223, 226–230, 232–234, 237, 239–240, 247, 249–250, 253
Jesus xiv, 17, 103, 153
Jewish people viii, 3, 5, 6, 8, 10–11, 13–18, 38–40, 52–55, 60, 62–63, 70, 72, 81–82, 103–104, 111–113, 115–119, 123–124, 131, 133, 147, 152, 159–162, 170–171, 175–179, 190–192, 195–199, 205, 213–214, 223, 225, 227, 231, 233, 249, 251
Jewish Quarter 14, 152, 159, 176
Jews 5–6, 10–11, 17–18, 20, 48, 54–55, 60, 63, 71, 82–83, 102, 110, 112–113, 115–116, 123–124, 129, 135, 138, 147, 152, 159–162, 176–178, 195–197, 213,

216, 223–224, 229–230, 233
jihad 17, 71, 83, 135, 146
jihad 17, 83, 130, 135, 146
jilbab 23
jizya 19, 138, 159
Johnston Plan 61
Jordan 2–3, 10, 31, 33, 41, 43, 48, 51, 55, 57, 61, 94–96, 105, 110–111, 113, 117–118, 121–122, 151–153, 155, 167, 169–170, 176, 196, 215, 218–219, 228
Jordan River 3, 57, 113, 170, 196
Jordan Valley 10, 61
Joseph's Tomb 14–15, 160
Judah 11, 101–102, 230, 253
Judaism 1, 151, 213
Judea and Samaria viii, 27, 50, 52, 55, 77, 81–82, 111, 147, 169
Justinian 13

K

Kabba 13
Karaites 5
Karens 117–118
Kashmir 50, 74, 135, 139, 147
Katanga 117
Kennedy, John F. 67
kharaj 159
Khomeini, Ayatollah Ruhollah 148
Khor al-Udaid 45
Khufu 164
Khuzistan 4, 27, 44, 139, 170
Kingdom of Jerusalem 103, 176

King David 54, 101, 175
King Farouk 31
King Hussein 48
King Solomon 10
Kissinger, Henry 83, 162
Knesset 62, 179
Kosovo 12, 15, 45, 93, 144, 149
Kurdistan 117, 218
Kurds 5, 43–44, 66, 118, 218
Kuwait 2–3, 6–7, 39, 43–47, 75, 96, 167, 193, 218

L

Land of Israel 10–11, 48, 82, 101–102, 124, 135, 138, 142, 169, 171, 178–179, 196
Last Supper 175
Law of Return 18
League of Nations 11, 111, 113, 156, 169, 198
Lebanon 2–4, 15, 21, 24, 28, 39, 41, 43–44, 47, 50–52, 57–58, 61, 70, 72, 80, 95–96, 100, 105, 124, 149, 155–156, 167, 198, 204–205, 215, 219, 240, 248
Libya 2–3, 14, 32–34, 43, 94–96, 139, 155, 167–168, 205, 216, 219
limited liability war 48
Line of Control 74
Luttwak, Edward N. 203

M

Macedonia 143–144, 149
Madrid Middle East Conference 162

Mahan, Alfred Thayer 94
Malaysia 76, 77, 148
Malta 141, 145
Mamelukes 11, 103
Mandaneans 5
Mandate 11, 103, 110–111, 113–114, 117, 123, 156, 169, 196, 198
Mandatory Palestine vii, 38, 107, 110–111, 113, 116, 156, 195, 198
Mandlebaum Gate 153
Maronites 5
Martel, Charles 12, 141
Masada 103
Mauritania 2, 97, 167
Mecca 13, 41, 43, 65, 84, 138, 178
Medina 19, 41, 65, 137–138
Mehmed II 14, 144
Menes 163
Middle East iii–iv, vii, x, xiii, 1–3, 5, 8, 10, 17, 27, 30, 38–40, 46–47, 50, 58, 64–65, 70, 78, 80–81, 84–85, 93–96, 99–100, 124, 141–142, 147, 162, 201–203, 206–208, 210, 215–216, 218, 222–226, 229, 232, 237–239, 243, 246–247, 253–254
Mikveh Yisrael 103
Min al-nahr ila al bahr 123
Mir Baki 14
misojudaism 55, 82–83
Mizos 117
Mongols 143
Montreux Convention 87

Moroccan Wall 74
Morocco 2, 6, 27, 34, 43, 67, 74, 96–97, 117–118, 155, 160, 167, 193, 205
Mount of Olives 8, 152, 161, 176
Mount Scopus 152–153
Moynihan, Daniel Patrick 58
Mubarak, Hosni 31
Mughal 14
Muhammad 19–20, 65, 79, 84, 130, 137–138, 140, 148–149, 161–162, 208, 210–212, 218
mujahadeen 148
Munich Olympics 51
Muslim Brotherhood 27, 50, 52
Myanmar 117, 192

N

Nagas 117
Nakhba 83
Narmer 163
Nasser, Gamal Abdel 6, 14, 28, 31, 34, 36, 39, 48, 50, 56, 66, 89, 182–183, 190
Nasserism 35
Near East vii, 2, 6–7, 93–96, 208, 224
Negev Desert 173
Nehemiah 54
Nestorians (Assyrians) 5
Nigeria 135, 146, 148
Nile River x, 1, 30, 139
niqab 23
Northern Kingdom of Israel 10
North Atlantic Treaty Organization 37

Nubia 140

O

occupations viii, x, 17, 157
Old City of Jerusalem 3, 104, 160
Oman 2, 34, 41–42, 45, 73–74, 76, 90–91, 96, 167, 193
Operation *Desert Storm* 47
Operation *Gatekeeper* 75
Operation *Hold the Line* 75
Operation *Thorns* 71
Organization of the Islamic Conference 40, 147
Orthodox 5, 12, 15, 135, 212
Oslo Accords 52, 61, 67, 71, 125
Ostland 171
Ottoman Turkey 12, 30–31, 38
Ottoman Turks 11, 13, 103, 143–145
Oval Office Bridge Plan 61

P

Pact of Khaybar 138
Pakistan 2, 40, 43, 74, 76, 95–97, 109, 135, 139, 147, 151, 169, 198
Palestina 171
Palestine vii, viii, x, 3, 6–8, 10, 17, 22, 27, 38, 40, 44, 50–51, 57, 60, 62–63, 67, 72, 82, 94–95, 103, 105, 107, 110–117, 121–126, 129–133, 153, 156, 167, 169, 195–196, 198–220, 225, 231–245, 247, 251
Palestine Liberation Front 51
Palestine Liberation Organization 8, 44, 50, 57, 67, 105, 121, 220
Palestinian Arabs 7, 14, 17–18, 39, 43, 46, 71, 82, 105, 110, 117–118, 122–123, 127–129, 156, 235
Palestinian Authority 52, 67, 71, 79, 118, 128
Palestinian National Covenant 8, 121, 124, 128–129
Pan-Arab unity x, 31, 34
Peel Commission 60, 107, 108
Pelagius of Asturias 140
Pelosi, Nancy 65
People's Democratic Republic of (South) Yemen 33–34, 73
Peres, Shimon 70
Perim Island 90
Persians 5, 11, 87
Persian Empire 30, 54
Persian Gulf 1, 4, 27, 75, 89–91, 94, 96, 170, 184, 220
Philippines 12, 135, 148
Philistines 101, 171
Phoenicians 1
Polisario 74
Pompey 103
Popular Front for the Liberation of Palestine 40, 51
Popular Front for the Liberation of Palestine-General Command 51
Popular Front for the Liberation of the Occupied Arab Gulf 42
population exchanges and transfers 6

Port Said 66
Prophet Joel 11
Protestant 5, 73
Ptolemaic Kingdom 30
Ptolemy 166

Q

Qadhafi, Muammar 28
Qassam, Abdel Karim 31
Qatar 2, 3, 45–46, 96, 167
Queen Nefertiti 165
Qur'an 19, 22, 24–25, 84, 159, 161–162, 177, 208, 247
Quraishi tribe 65

R

Rabbinical Jews 5
Rabbi Akiva Ben Joseph 54
Rabbi Ashi 15
Rabbi Lieberman, Hillel 15
Rabin, Yitzhak 70
Rachel's Tomb 16, 77
Radafan uprising 42
Rama 14
Ramses II 166
Ras Mussandam Peninsula 90
Reconquista 140, 143
Red Sea 45, 84, 90
refugee problem 6–7, 202
Rhodes Armistice 61
Rice, Condolezza 65
Road Map 62
Romans 11, 54, 103, 171
Roman Catholics 5
Rumailah oilfields 46
Ruus al Jibal 90

S

Sadat, Anwar el- 31, 52, 62–64, 68–69
Saharawis 117
Said, Nuri as- 31
Saiqa 51
salaam 70
Saladin 143
Samaria viii, 8, 10, 27, 39, 50, 52, 55, 61, 70, 77, 81–82, 102, 104, 110–111, 113, 118–119, 121–122, 147, 155–157, 160, 169, 171, 173, 231, 250
Samaritans 5
San Remo conference 111
Saudi Arabia 2–3, 6–7, 12, 24, 36, 41–43, 45–46, 75–77, 95–96, 167, 198, 221
Sea of Marmara 87
Second Lebanon War 57–58, 80, 149, 203
Second Temple 83, 102–103
security barriers 16, 73
Security Fence Act 75
Seleucid Kingdom 30
Seljuks 11
Serbia 12, 93, 144, 171
settlements 7–8, 61, 82
Shabaka 5
shaheed 82
Shamir, Yitzhak 179
Sharia 22–23, 135
Sharm el-Sheikh 76
Shatt al-Arab 1, 41, 66
Shchem 14, 27, 82, 101, 160
Shiite 12, 15, 36, 45, 52

Sinai 11, 36, 48–49, 52, 56, 61, 66, 76, 89–90, 95, 104, 155, 157, 203, 219, 222, 235–236
Sinai-Suez War 36, 56, 66, 89–90, 95, 104, 203
Six Day War 8, 50, 57, 61, 81, 89–90, 104, 121–122, 203, 236, 251
Sobieski, Jan III 12, 145
Solomon's Stables 15
Somalia 12, 43, 167
South Kasai 117
Soviet Union 53, 66, 73, 96, 100, 108–109, 148, 155, 189–190, 192, 197, 224–225, 230, 239
Sri Lanka 117, 192
Sudan 2–3, 32, 34, 41, 44–46, 61, 96, 117, 135, 140, 146, 148, 161, 167, 216, 221
Suez Canal viii, x, 1, 49, 56, 66, 69, 88–89, 181–183, 185–186
Sulawesi 149
sulha 70
Sumerians 1
sumuh 64
Sunni 12, 52
suras 19, 20, 21
Syria 2–5, 31–33, 39, 43–44, 47, 50, 55, 57–58, 70, 94–96, 105, 113, 118–119, 138, 142–144, 155–157, 167, 198, 205, 215, 222
Syrian Catholics 5

T

Taba Talks 61
Tajikistan 2, 45, 97
talaq 24
Tanzim 50
taqiyya (deception) 65–66, 68–69
Temple Mount 13, 15, 16, 27, 54, 139, 178, 250
Texas 75, 119
Thailand 12, 77, 135, 192, 198
Third Crusade 143
Thutmose II 165
Tibet 117, 155
Tigris x, 1, 30
Tigris-Euphrates x, 1, 30
Timor Este (East Timor) 43, 148
Tiran 1, 56–57, 66, 90
Tisha B'Av 178
Tours, France 12
Trans-Jordan 94–95, 113, 167, 169–170
Treaty of
  1533 145
  Al-Hudaybiyya 65, 137
  Craiova 108
  Israel-Egypt Peace 104
  Israel-Jordan Peace 61, 105
  Israel-Lebanon 61
  Kuchuk Kainarji 146
  Passorowitz 146
Tripoli 14
Tunb Island 91
Tunisia 2, 33, 71, 96, 140, 167–168, 193, 205
Turkey 2, 4, 12–14, 30–31, 36–38, 40, 43, 49, 74, 87–88, 94–96, 107, 109, 147–148,

155, 157, 181, 183, 189, 192, 198, 224
Turkomans 5
Turks 5, 11–12, 14, 103, 107, 109, 142–147
Tutankhamun III 165

U

U Thant 56
UN General Assembly Resolution viii, 59, 192, 196
U.N. Partition plan for Palestine 40
Uighurs 117
Umar 138–139, 142
Umayyads 139, 141
umma 24, 78, 138
United Arab Emirates 2, 33, 35, 76, 91, 96, 167, 219
United Arab Republic 31–32, 34, 41, 68, 96, 100
United Arab States 31
United Kingdom 7, 48, 88–89, 169, 183–184, 198
United Nations viii, 6–7, 11, 15, 48, 55–58, 60–61, 66–68, 74, 95, 104, 113–114, 123, 157, 162, 169, 189, 191–192, 196, 201, 247
United Nations Emergency Force 48, 56, 66
United Nations General Assembly 58, 104, 123, 162, 189
United Nations High Commissioner for Refugees 7
United Nations Mission for a Referendum in Western Sahara 67

United Nations Relief and Works Agency for Palestine Refugees in the Near East 6–7
United Nations Truce Supervisory Organization 55
United States iv, 6–7, 12, 17, 26, 48, 66, 71, 75, 83, 91, 99, 116, 119, 126, 149, 162, 177, 184, 187, 189, 191–192, 197, 223, 225, 253–254
UN General Assembly Resolution 181 196
UN General Assembly Resolution 3379 59
UN General Assembly Resolution 46/86 192
Upper Galilee 173
uswa hasana 162
U Thant 56
Uthman 139

V

Vienna, Austria 12, 145
Vikramasli temple 13
Virgin Mary 175
Vishnu 14

W

Wahhabist 12
Waqf 16, 130
Warbah and Bubiyan 46
Weizmann-Suleiman Bey Nassir understanding 60
Western Sahara 27, 43, 67, 74, 155
Western Wall 83, 152–153, 176

Woodhead Commission 60
World War I 37–38, 49, 53, 87, 94, 107, 116
Wye River Memorandum 67, 105

Y

Yemen 2, 31–35, 42–45, 47, 73, 76, 95–96, 161, 167–168, 198, 205, 216, 222
Yezids 5
Yishuv 38
Yom Kippur War 52, 69, 83, 89–90, 104, 238, 239

Z

Zanzibar 42, 146
Zionism viii, 53–55, 59, 82, 103, 122, 131, 133, 189–190, 193, 214, 229, 249
Zionism is Racism Resolution 59
Ziyad, Tariq ibn 12, 140
Zoroastrians 5
zunar 162